D1236945

O the mind, mind has mountains; cliffs of fall
Frightful, sheer, no-man-fathomed. Hold them cheap
May who ne'er hung there. Nor does long our small
Durance deal with that steep or deep.

CLIFFS OF FALL

*Paradox and Polyvalence
in the Parables of Jesus*

JOHN DOMINIC CROSSAN

A Crossroad Book

THE SEABURY PRESS / NEW YORK

For Bel and George

1980
The Seabury Press
815 Second Avenue/New York, N.Y. 10017

Library of Congress Cataloging in Publication Data
Crossan, John Dominic.   Cliffs of fall.
"A Crossroad book."
Bibliography: p.
Includes index.
1. Jesus Christ—Parables—Addresses, essays,
lectures.   I.   Title.
BT375.2.C75   226'.8'06   79-24824
ISBN 0-8164-0113-6

Grateful acknowledgment is made to Oxford University Press for
permission to quote from *The Poems of Gerard Manley Hopkins,*
ed. W. H. Gardiner and N. H. Mackenzie, Poems © The
Society of Jesus 1967; and to A. R. Ammons for permission to
quote from his following books: *Expressions of Sea Level,*
copyright © 1957, 1959, 1960, 1962, 1963 by A. R. Ammons;
Corsons Inlet, copyright © 1965 by Cornell University; *Tape for
the Turn of the Year,* copyright © 1965 by Cornell University;
and *Sphere: The Form of a Motion,* copyright © 1974 by A. R.
Ammons.

CONTENTS

PREFACE

Let me now
{ Jolt
{ Shake and unset your morticed metaphors.
Gerard Manley Hopkins
(*Gardner and MacKenzie: 142*)

The three chapters of this book were all written for and delivered in other situations than their present unified location. They are reprinted with editorial permission.

The first chapter, "Paradox and Metaphor," was originally entitled "Paradox Gives Rise to Metaphor: Paul Ricoeur's Hermeneutics and the Parables of Jesus." It was given on November 11, 1978, as part of a symposium on "Paul Ricoeur and Biblical Hermeneutics" for a meeting of the Chicago Society of Biblical Research. It was published in that society's journal, *Biblical Research,* for 1979–1980.

The second chapter, "Sower and Seed," was originally entitled "Sower and Seed: Univalence and Polyvalence in Hermeneutics." It was prepared under the general rubric of "The Bible and the Hermeneutical Task" for The William Rainey Harper Conference on Biblical Studies at the Divinity School of the University of Chicago on October 3–5, 1979. It is published here for the first time.

The third chapter, "Polyvalence and Play," was originally entitled "A Metamodel for Polyvalent Narration." It was written for and published in *Semeia* 9 (1977): *Polyvalent Narration.*

Only very minor changes or additions have been made in the texts of the original versions. Since they all explore the same general problem of paradox and polyvalence in the parables of Jesus, I have preferred to leave them more or less as they were, as the cries of their several and separate occasions.

One

PARADOX AND METAPHOR

If we are right in saying that one can only think of a
thing by thinking of it as something, how are we to
think of it in that initial phase when we are still making
up our minds what to think of it as?

(Sparshott: 78)

In this discussion I shall be primarily concerned with the
essays by Paul Ricoeur in *Semeia* 4 (1975) but I shall be
considering them in the light of his more recent works
(1976, 1977, 1978).

Paul Ricoeur has defined parable by noting that "the
parable, it seems to me, is the conjunction of a *narrative
form* and a *metaphorical process.* Later I shall add a third
decisive trait" (1975:30). At that later moment he com-
pletes the definition with these words: "Let me first summarize the three traits which seem to me essential to the
definition of the 'literary genre' of the parable: the narrative parable relies on the conjunction between a *narrative
form,* a *metaphorical process,* and an appropriate 'qualifier'
which insures its convergence with other forms of discourse which all point toward the meaning 'Kingdom of
God' " (1975:33).

You will notice immediately that the first two elements
are relatively easy to fix linguistically since "narrative
form" and "metaphorical process" are repeated, italicized,

and then used as titles for the first two essays. The third element is much harder to explain and several different phrases and terms are used concerning it: extravagance, oddness, radicality (1975:32–33). I would summarize the three elements of Ricoeur's definition, in my own words, as: narrativity, metaphoricity, paradoxicality.

There is, however, one much more important point to be noted in this definition. In the context of the *Semeia* volume the term "parables" was really a contextually legitimate shorthand for Jesus' parables of the Kingdom of God. Outside that context it is necessary to distinguish between (1) parables in general, and (2) Jesus' parables in particular. These two headings will serve to organize my own comments.

1. PARABLES

If I understand him correctly, Paul Ricoeur would define the literary genre of parable as the combination of narrative form and metaphorical process. Using the term "parable" in the wider generic sense which would have to include, for instance, Zen parables as well as Jewish ones, and which would have to extend from Jesus and the Rabbis, among the ancients, to Kafka, Borges, and Calvino, among the moderns, the two major elements are metaphoricity and narrativity.

I would suggest that a third element is also necessary for the genre's definition, and then add some comments on the other two proposed elements.

1.1 Brevity

This is the third necessary element in the generic definition of parable. *Parable is a very short metaphorical narrative.* Two arguments help to support this position.

1.11 Borges and Brevity

The first argument is taken from the theory and even more from the practice of the poet-parabler Jorge Luis Borges (Crossan, 1976:88). In the "Prologue" for his 1941 collection of stories, *Ficciones,* Borges laughed at those who wanted "to go on for five hundred pages developing an idea whose perfect oral expression is possible in a few minutes" (1962:15). Thirty years later, in a note of commentary on "The Maker," a story in his collection entitled *The Aleph,* he would still assert the value of brevity. "Ever since 1934, the writing of short prose pieces—fables, parables, brief narratives—has given me a certain mysterious satisfaction. I think of such pages as these as I think of coins—small material objects, hard and bright, tokens of something else" (1971:202). Borges can criticize Kafka on precisely this point. In conversation with Richard Burgin he says somewhat caustically: "I mean, when you've read the first page of *The Trial* you know that he'll never know why he's being judged, why he's being tried. . . ." This means that "though his stories may be parables of the subject, still they're not written by him to be parables" (Burgin: 60).

1.12 Schwartz and Brevity

My second argument comes from another poet-parabler, Howard Schwartz. He has edited a magnificent anthology of modern parables and in an "Afterword" he has argued that, "due primarily to the rigid classifications of literary genres, which for most readers limit the possibilities to the short story, the novel, lyric and epic poetry, and drama, the modern parable has so far failed to receive recognition as an independent literary form. Yet now that so many authors have successfully written in this allegorical mode, it is obvious that the parable has been resurrected as a literary genre" (Schwartz: 320). In a review of this book for *Parabola* in Winter, 1977 (128), and in summarizing his conclusions, I gave his generic definition of parable as "an allegorical narrative of minimal length." There are thus three elements in a parable. First, brevity. "The basic challenge of the parable is to write a good story in as short a space as possible" (Schwartz: xix). Again: "Because most of these works are too short to be called short stories, the term 'mini-story' has been proposed" (Schwartz: 320). Second, narrativity. "The modern parable, more often than not, presents a recognizable narrative" (Schwartz: 321). This distinguishes it from dreams on the one hand and prose poems on the other. Third, allegory. "The key literary device of both the ancient and modern parable, that of allegory, presumes a double meaning, that presented and that implied" (Schwartz: 326). It is very easy to correlate Schwartz's terms "narrative" and "allegory" with Ricoeur's terms "narrative form" and "metaphorical process," especially since Ricoeur has suggested that "the opposition between 'allegorical interpretation' and metaphorical interpretation must be submitted to scrutiny and maybe to revision" (1975:35). Metaphor and allegory may not be as antithetical as we have tended to think since the time of Coleridge.

If all this is correct, *brevity* (as short as possible) is an element in the generic definition of parable and will demand eventually as much attention as *narrativity* and *metaphoricity*. For the moment I shall only point to one result of including it within the generic definition of parable. It may well answer Ricoeur's question concerning how we discern the narrative's metaphoricity in a parable (1975:98). That is, how, apart from context, do we know that the parable of The Sower is not just a simple agricultural lesson on proper and improper techniques for improving one's harvest? Apart from contextual clues, it may well be the very brevity of the narrative that first impels us

to look elsewhere for its fullest meaning. Adapting Borges'
image of the parable as coin, it is clear that coins are small
because they point elsewhere, their true content is always
somewhere else.

1.2 Metaphoricity

I am in rather complete agreement with Ricoeur's second parabolic element: metaphoric process or metaphoricity. But it is at this point that the much more radical and
provocative view of metaphor which has appeared in *The
Rule of Metaphor* (1977) must be added to the discussion.

1.21 *The Paradox of Metaphor*

I would like to cite three fairly long passages from that
recently translated book, one towards the start, a second
near the middle, and the last one towards the end of that
volume. Their length, repetition, and location indicate
how important metaphor's ineluctable necessity and inevitable rule over us has become for Ricoeur.

(a) *Literal and figurative language.* The first citation
questions the security of the distinction between proper or
literal and figurative or metaphorical language in favor of
the original metaphoricity of all language (1977:22–23).

> If metaphor belongs to an heuristic of thought, could
> we not imagine that the process that disturbs and dis-
> places a certain logical order, a certain conceptual
> hierarchy, a certain classification scheme, is the same as
> that from which all classification proceeds? Certainly,
> the only functioning of language we are aware of oper-
> ates within an already constituted order; metaphor
> does not produce a new order except by creating rifts
> in an old order. Nevertheless, could we not imagine
> that the order itself is born in the same way that it
> changes? Is there not, in Gadamer's terms, a
> 'metaphoric' at work at the origin of logical thought, at
> the root of all classification? This is a more far-reaching

hypothesis than the others, which presuppose an already constituted language within which metaphor operates. Not only is the notion of deviation linked to this presupposition, but also the opposition between 'ordinary' language and 'strange' or 'rare' language, which Aristotle himself introduced, as well as, most definitely, the opposition introduced later between 'proper' and 'figurative.' The idea of an initial metaphorical impulse destroys these oppositions between proper and figurative, ordinary and strange, order and transgression. It suggests the idea that order itself proceeds from the metaphorical constitution of semantic fields, which themselves give rise to genus and species.

(b) *The search for literal language.* These next lines go beyond the hypothetical presentation of the preceding challenge and assert the unavailability of this language-other-than-metaphorical, this non-figurative, non-metaphorical, literal, and proper language (1977:138).

> Everyone agrees in saying that figurative language exists only if one can contrast it with another language that is not figurative. There is even agreement on this point with the English-language semanticists. As we saw, a metaphorical word functions only when it is contrasted and combined with other non-metaphorical words (Max Black); the self-contradiction of literal interpretation is necessary for the unfolding of metaphorical interpretation (Monroe Beardsley). What, then, is this other language, unmarked from the rhetorical point of view? One must first admit that it cannot be found.

Two other philosophers have recently raised similar doubts about this "proper" language. Karsten Harries has said that "ever since Aristotle, metaphor . . . is an improper naming. This impropriety invites a movement of interpretation that can come to rest only when metaphorical has been replaced with a more proper speech. This is not to say, however, that such replacement is possible nor that interpretation can ever come to rest" (74). And W. V. Quine has also reminded us that "it is a mistake, then, to think of linguistic usage as literalistic in its main body and metaphorical in its trimming. Metaphor, or something like it, governs both the growth of language and our acquisition of it. What comes as a subsequent refinement is rather cognitive discourse itself, at its most drably literal. The neatly worked out inner stretches of science are an open space in the tropical jungle, created by clearing tropes away" (162).

(c) *The auto-implication of metaphor.* Finally, the third citation affirms all this emphatically, and in terms of paradox (1977:286–87).

> The final product of this effectiveness of worn-out metaphor, which is thus replaced by the production of a concept that erases its trace, is that discourse on metaphor is itself infected by the universal metaphoricity of philosophical discourse. In this regard, one can speak of a paradox of the auto-implication of metaphor.
>
> The paradox is this: there is no discourse on metaphor that is not stated within a metaphorically engendered conceptual network. There is no metaphorical standpoint from which to perceive the order and the demarcation of the metaphorical field. Metaphor is metaphorically stated. The word *metaphor* and the word *figure* alike attest to this recurrence of metaphor. The theory of metaphor returns in a circular manner to the metaphor of theory, which determines the truth of being in terms of presence. If this is so, there can then be no principle for delimiting metaphor, no definition in which the defining does not contain the defined; metaphoricity is absolutely uncontrollable.

With that last citation we have come a long way indeed from metaphor fighting for its life and validity against or beside the proposed normalcy and universality of proper, literal, or scientific language (see also Ricoeur, 1978:145).

1.22 The Ubiquity of Metaphor

I would like to make five comments on the passages just cited and especially on that final one.

(a) *Metaphor and religious language.* First, if this view of metaphor's universality is correct, and I think that it is, anyone invoking metaphorical, symbolical, or figurative language as somehow peculiarly appropriate for religious discussions and divine descriptions would have to rethink and reground that position.

(b) *Metaphor and translation.* Second, it now becomes much clearer why we can and must claim that metaphor is untranslatable. It is certainly possible, in a specific case, to deconstruct and analyze how a metaphor works and to translate it to that extent. But every metaphor, save the momentarily jaded or temporarily dormant, is but a localized indication and instance of the ultimate ubiquity and radical universality of metaphor itself. That is, any given metaphor is but a metonym for the primordial metaphoricity of language. And that means, I suppose, that there is only metonym, rather than metaphor, in the final analysis.

(c) *Metaphor and univalence.* Third, none of this denies that in certain cases and situations we may wish to render a given speech as univalent and literal as possible. But language is intrinsically not on our side in such perfectly legitimate endeavors. It is not that our language is normally or intrinsically univalent and only the perversity of poets and the deviance of novelists render it polyvalent. Language, because of the act of arbitrary convention at its heart, is intrinsically polyvalent and only our careful endeavors or our most indifferent occasions render it univalent. Think, for instance, of what would happen to our nice, literal, univocal, and univalent red octagonal stop sign if a certain dissenting group chose it as their banner.

(d) *Metaphor and absence.* Fourth, you will notice two phrases in my final citation from Ricoeur: "erases its trace" and "being in terms of presence." In my own thinking about metaphor I have found myself forced into this much more radical view between *In Parables* (1973) and *Raid on the Articulate* (1976) primarily from the work of another French philosopher, Jacques Derrida. And it is precisely Derrida whose echoes one hears in words such as: erasure, trace (positively), and presence (negatively). Derrida has insisted that Western philosophy has always operated as an indefensible philosophy of *presence* and resolutely refused to face the absence which was its ground. Two quotations will have to suffice, both from the excellent introduction to his thought given by Gayatri Chakravorty Spivak in *Of Grammatology* (Derrida, 1976:xvii).

> Derrida suggests that what opens the possibility of thought is not merely the question of being, but also the never-annulled difference from 'the completely other.' Such is the strange 'being' of the sign: half of it always 'not there' and the other half always 'not that.' The structure of the sign is determined by the trace or track of that other which is forever absent. . . .
>
> Heidegger's Being might point at an inarticulable presence. Derrida's trace is the mark of the absence of a presence, an always already absent present, of the lack at the origin that is the condition of thought and experience.

In terms of metaphor this would mean that it is precisely the *absence* of a fixed, literal, univocal, or univalent language that releases the inevitability and universality of metaphor itself. And this absence is the foundation and horizon of all language and of all thought. If Derrida is correct in this challenge, and I think that he is, it would mean that metaphor or symbol does not so much have a "surplus of meaning," in Ricoeur's phrase (1976), as a *void of meaning* at its core. Like a Rorschach, it can mean so many things and generate so many differing interpretations because it has no fixed, univocal, or absolute meaning to begin with. That is why it is inexhaustible. Thus, Karsten Harries is more in agreement with Derrida than with Ricoeur when he says that, "Metaphor speaks of what remains absent. All metaphor that is more than an abbreviation for more proper speech gestures towards what transcends language. Thus metaphor implies lack. God knows neither transcendence nor metaphor—nor would man, if he were truly godlike. The refusal of metaphor is inseparably connected with the project of pride, the dream of an unmediated vision, a vision that is not marred by lack, that does not refer to something beyond itself that would fulfill it" (84).

(e) *Metaphor and negative theology.* Fifth, both Derrida and his translator just cited insist that none of this has anything to do with theology, "not even in the most negative order of negative theology" (Derrida, 1973:104; 1976:lxxi, lxxviii, 71, 98). Or, again, "Just as there is a negative theology, there is a negative atheology. An accomplice of the former, it still pronounces the absence of a center, when it is play that should be affirmed. But is not the desire for a center, as a function of play itself, the indestructible itself? And in the repetition and return of play, how could the phantom of center not call to us? It is here that the hesitation between writing as decentering and writing as an affirmation of play is infinite" (1978:297). But surely all this depends on how one understands negative theology, on how one proposes the *via negativa* in a modern translation and, for me at least, what Derrida is saying leads straight into a contemporary retrieval of negative theology, that is, of course, a theology articulating itself by a philosophy of absence. And if one wishes to see this at work in terms of practical exegesis, one can hardly do better than to *re*consider the analyses of Matthew 13 and Mark 16 by Louis Marin noted by Paul Ricoeur in *Semeia* 4 (1975:54–63).

1.23 *The Source of Metaphor*

I shall conclude this section on metaphoricity with three metaphors from Italo Calvino's book *The Castle of Crossed Destinies* (37–39).

If Moon is not-Earth, how should one construe that otherness? Does Moon contain things *different* from Earth, or does it contain the *opposite* of the things of Earth, or, finally, does it contain the *absence* of all the things of Earth?

The first answer is that in "the pale fields of the Moon . . . an endless storeroom preserves in phials placed in rows . . . the stories that men do not live, the thoughts that knock once at the threshold of awareness and vanish forever, the particles of the possible discarded in the game of combinations, the solutions that could be reached but are never reached."

The second answer is that "the world of the moon . . . would allow us to indulge in the old fancies of an upside-down world, where the ass is king, man is four legged, the young rules the old, sleepwalkers hold the rudder, citizens spin like squirrels in their cage's wheel, and there are as many other paradoxes as the imagination can disjoin and join."

But, finally, there is the third answer and it is "the poet's reply" which ends the debate. "No, the Moon is a desert. . . . From this arid sphere every discourse and every poem sets forth; and every journey through forests, battles, treasures, banquets, bedchambers, brings us back here, to the center of the empty horizon."

1.3 Narrativity

The third element in the definition of the literary genre of parable is narrativity and here, it seems to me, all the questions from the preceding section repeat themselves in barely changed format.

1.31 Narrative and Metaphor

Since, for Ricoeur, a "narrative form" can be joined to a "metaphorical process," could this mean that narrativity might be just as humanly ubiquitous and ineluctable as metaphoricity itself? And could this universality be but a different aspect of the same human inevitability? In other words, was I going too far to claim in *The Dark Interval* that "we live in story like fish in the sea"? (Crossan, 1975:47).

1.32 Narrative and World

Professor Ricoeur has always insisted on the referential dimensions of language, that language and narrative bespeak a world. With this I am in complete agreement. But when, for example, one accepts the absolute rule of metaphor and agrees that such terms as literal, univocal, or non-metaphorical language designate only a *con*vention (pun intended) within total metaphoricity, a section such as his "Metaphor and Reality" in *Semeia* 4 will need serious revision (1975:80–88).

The question is *not* (1) does narrative have reference to world and reality? To that question I would offer an emphatic affirmative. But the question is (2) does narrative refer to a world and a reality that it itself has created and which without it is humanly incomprehensible and unintelligible, is just the humming buzz of meaningless sense impressions? Tactically and polemically one may insist that language refers only to linguisticality, metaphor to metaphoricity, or narrative to narrativity, but what is meant, I would think, is: (1) *not* that language refers only to language, *but* (2) that language refers only to linguistic world. The real issue between existential phenomenology and linguistic structuralism lies there—not in setting existence against language or world against metaphor or reality against narrative, but in facing the ultimate implications of a radically linguistic existence, a radically metaphorical world, and a radically narrative existence. Or, in other words, if, as Paul Ricoeur claims, reality is *re*described by poetic fictions, by what was it described in the first place?

2. JESUS' PARABLES

Paul Ricoeur has made three important qualifications on his general definition of parable in discussing the usage of Jesus.

2.1 Limitation

Since the specificity of religious language consists in processes of "intensification, transgression, and going to the limit," Ricoeur gathers "these diverse procedures under the general title of 'limit-expressions' " (1975:107). This means that no particular genre or linguistic form is intrinsically religious as such. It becomes religious, becomes language about God, through what Ricoeur wishes "provisionally [to] call the 'transgression' by which these forms of discourse point beyond their immediate signification toward the Wholly Other" (1975:108).

This means that such processes of "transgression" wherein expressions become "limit-expressions" will appear across all the genres of Jesus' speech and all the forms of Jesus' language in so far as these are religious, are about the Kingdom of God. And, of course, "transgression" may also be expected in his deeds as well as in his words.

In so far as the parables of Jesus are religious discourse, then, Ricoeur finds that here "the limit-expression [is] constituted by the extravagance of the parables" (1975:114). He means that "the parables tell stories that could have happened, but it is this realism of situations, characters and plots that precisely heightens the eccentricity of the modes of behavior to which the Kingdom of heaven is compared. The *extraordinary in the ordinary:* this is what strikes me in the dénouement of the parables" (1975:115).

2.2 Paradox

I am in complete agreement with this and the three comments I wish to make on it intend only to sharpen and intensify the implications of his thesis. I shall use the general expression "paradox" or "paradoxicality" as my own general term to include the full spectrum of phenomena which Ricoeur subsumes under nouns such as hyperbole, paradox, limit-expression, etc., or adjectives such as strange, radical, extravagant, etc.

2.21 The Existence of Paradox

In so far as we are concerned with Jesus' parables, that is, with the reconstruction of the parables of the historical Jesus, a careful separation of the layers of tradition will be necessary before one decides where exactly such hyperbolic, paradoxical, and extravagant limit-expressions are to be found. If it is correct to claim, as I would, that Jesus spoke of God in paradoxical parables but that the tradition spoke of Jesus as the Paradoxical Parable of God, this could mean, in Ricoeur's terms, that Jesus' *religious* parables were thus freed to become the tradition's *theological* parables. In such a quite legitimate transition many "trans-gressions" may have been generated less as religious paradox than as the precipitate of generic or thematic change or as the result of simple transmissional awkward-ness.

One example will suffice. In a very interesting recent article on "Atypical Features in the Parables of Jesus," Norman A. Huffman notes paradox in Jesus' story "about a particular mustard seed which—mirabile dictu—became a tree!" (212). I also would see paradox in The Mustard Seed parable but elsewhere, and indeed, a far more radical paradox than this suggestion. Instead of likening God's Kingdom to the cedar of Lebanon as the great arboreal eschatological image, Jesus has satirized this mighty metaphor by reducing it from giant cedar to humble mus-tard plant, as Robert Funk has already argued. But the tradition is busily bringing this image into more standard eschatological viewpoints, converting it from plant or shrub back into tree, and thus producing a rather unfortu-nate combination, especially in Matthew. I do not find it prudent to press further this Matthean combination of Mark 4:32 (shrub) and Q/Luke 13:19 (tree) into "it is the greatest of shrubs and becomes a tree" (Matt 13:32). It is, I suppose, a rather accidental paradox and should be han-dled with the same delicacy with which one handles that other masterful Matthean combination in 21:5–7 where, from Zechariah 9:9 and Mark 14:7, he has created this: "The disciples went and did as Jesus had directed them; they brought the ass and the colt, and put their garments on *them* [*ep' ayton*] and he sat thereon [lit., "on them," *epano ayton*]. The image of Jesus riding astride two animals should not be pressed as divine paradox and neither, I would suggest, should that of the shrub which "becomes" a tree. The point of all this is that *history of transmission must precede assertion of paradox* in the parables of Jesus.

2.22 The Extent of Paradox

Although I agree with most of the instances of "extravagance" itemized by Ricoeur in the parables of Jesus, as well as most of the "atypical" elements noted by Huffman in the article just discussed, I would prefer to enlarge the scope of such paradoxicality as widely as possible. This means that it would not depend just on this or that item within a parable which might be argued this way or that, which might be argued towards normalcy or towards extravagance.

The full extent of Jesus' paradoxicality can be outlined under three simultaneous rubrics borrowed, primarily for their organizational usefulness, from American semiotic theory. Paradoxical aspects are evinced by Jesus' parables in terms of their pragmatics, their semantics, and their syntactics.

(a) *The pragmatics of Jesus' parables.* By this term I mean all that pertains to the relationship between Jesus and his audience. Chastened by past disaster, most scholars are reluctant to imagine or discuss the pragmatics of Jesus' parables. Even if much of the evangelical reaction to them is later creation, was there no conversation and discussion, no questions and answers, in the original historical situation? Or, as Huffman has recently suggested, should we imagine that Jesus "made use of the actor's skills to convince his audiences?" (220).

Despite the immense lacunae in our historical information on such points, I would suggest three aspects of parabolic pragmatics that were, especially in their conjunction, paradoxical and provocative in themselves, even before moving on to the syntactics or semantics of his stories.

The offical teachers of Jesus' day taught: (1) within a group authority; (2) within an official synagogue; (3) within a "canonical" text. Jesus, on the other hand, taught: (1) outside this group authority; (2) outside the synagogue by the lakeside; (3) outside the "canonical" texts. Indeed, it is almost as if his parables displaced the scriptures as text. Authority, situation or setting, and "text" for teaching are all paradoxically different with Jesus. This is before and apart from whatever is contained within the parables themselves.

(b) *The semantics of Jesus' parables.* It has been customary, since Bultmann and Jeremias, to compare certain parables of Jesus with similar ones from rabbinical sources. One usually presumes that these other parables were available at the time of Jesus and were known to both him and his audience. Such comparisons are extremely useful in terms of synchronic comparison but only in terms of such since it seems certain that the rabbinical examples were created, diachronically, at a later date.

In his magisterial work on the Pharisaic traditions before 70 C.E., Jacob Neusner has nothing on parables (1971). And in criticizing Bultmann's comparison of Jesus' parables with ones non-existent in his period, he has said (1972:376):

> As to similitudes and similar forms, we find no equivalent. To be sure, we do see the use of paradox in some apophthegms, such as *Hanina/lizard;* but paradox is not a dominant characteristic of the Pharisaic-rabbinic sayings and does not occur in stories as the primary vehicle for narrative. Hyperbole and metaphors are not common. As to such similitudes as *servant/master, tower/war, lost sheep/lost coin,* the thief, faithful servant, children at play, leaven, seed growing of itself, treasure in the field, pearl of great price, fish net, house builder, fig tree, returning householder, prodigal son, unjust steward, two sons, and the like—we have nothing of the same sort. It is true that later rabbinic materials make use of similitudes. But the Pharisaic stratum is notably lacking in them. Bultmann's rabbinic parallels are all from masters after 70.

This means that, as with the pragmatics of situation and setting, so also with the basic semantics of Jesus' stories, we are already within a most unusual phenomenon. Thus the specific itemizing of atypical or extravagant items, even taken cumulatively, must be understood against this even more fundamental linguistic originality and generic creativity.

(c) *The syntactics of Jesus' parables.* Robert M. Johnston (1976:337) has published a section of his doctoral dissertation on parables "as ascribed to Tannaim (scribes and rabbis who flourished ca. C.E. 220)." He gives the immediate contextual and textual structure of their "typical narrative *mashal*" as follows (1976:342):

1. Illustrand (the point to be illustrated);
2. Introductory formula, whether full or abbreviated;
3. The parable proper (*Bildhälfte*);
4. Application, usually introduced by *kai* or equivalent link-word or phrase;
5. Scripture quotation, often introduced by "as it is said" or "as it is written."

As he well knows, and as we have just seen, this form is much later than the Pharisaic stratum contemporary with Jesus and cannot be used legitimately as a source or cause for Jesus' parables in any diachronic or genetic sense. Any comparison, from Jesus' point of view, can only be generic or synchronic and it is only in this sense that the rabbinical parables in Fiebig and Jülicher, Bultmann and Jeremias, Strack and Billerbeck may still be used.

My present point presumes all that and is intended as an indication of how, in the light of *subsequent* rabbinical parables after his period, one might have expected the syntactics of Jesus' parabolic presentation to have appeared. What is evident is that point (1), the illustrand, is usually the Kingdom of God, that is, the mystery of God's relations with ourselves, and not a moral problem or a scriptural difficulty. And while points (2) and (3) from Johnston's schema for the later period appear also in Jesus' format, the absence of points (4) and (5) is very striking, especially since the Christian transmission tends to add them to the original parables. In other words, despite or even because of the transmission's addition of application, what is most strikingly absent in the original syntactics of Jesus' parables is precisely this clear terminal application and explanation. One seldom has any doubts about the meaning of a rabbinical parable in context but the exact opposite seems to be the case with Jesus. It is surely good to know that talents should be used and oil conserved but it would be even better to be certain what talents actually mean and what oil actually represents. Poised syntactically between illustrand and application, and hedged carefully by prior and subsequent biblical citation, there is seldom any doubt about the meaning of the later rabbinical parables. The opposite seems true for Jesus.

My point in all this is that the paradoxicality of Jesus' parables does not just depend on this or that extravagant item within each one. It extends to their entire pragmatics, semantics, and syntactics, and only against this wider background should any isolated item, or even all such items, be stressed as extravagant, atypical, or paradoxical. This would also mean that, in Ricoeur's distinction, Jesus' stories are *religious parables* while most of the (later) rabbinical stories are *theological parables*.

2.23 *The Function of Paradox*

In my last two sections (2.21; 2.22) I intended only to intensify and expand the arguments of Ricoeur on the extravagance or paradoxicality of Jesus' stories. My next three sections intend to raise questions for further and future discussion, presuming the validity of those preceding points.

(a) *Paradox and aniconicity.* Paradoxicality seems to riddle the words and deeds of Jesus, the style and substance, the form and content of his speech. What is the function of such insistent radicality, such reiterated paradoxicality? Or, in Ricoeur's terms, if we agree that religious language is limit-language, why is that so?

For now I shall simply raise the question and indicate where I have tried elsewhere to answer it. I have argued in *Raid on the Articulate* (1976) and also in a recent volume in Semeia Supplements (1979) that Jesus' paradoxicality is the result of turning the aniconicity of Israel's God onto language itself, onto the very forms and content of human speech. Jesus' language is simply language genuflecting before Israel's aniconic God.

I would argue that scholarship has discussed Israel too much in terms of monotheism against polytheism and not at all enough in terms of aniconic against iconic monotheism. What does it do to the human imagination to imagine an unimaginable God? Is it possible to proclaim figural aniconicity and still assert linguistic iconicity? Must not iconicity, however long it may take, turn eventually on language itself?

It is, I would maintain, with the Jewish Jesus that the Jewish tradition forced the aniconicity of God onto the surface of language itself and, with inevitable paradox, announced that God could no more be trapped in the forms and genres of linguistic art than in the shapes and figures of plastic art.

(b) *Paradox and politics.* In a review of my own book *Raid on the Articulate,* John H. Elliott has noted that its "implications . . . are social and sociological as well as philosophical and theological" but that on such things as "social interaction, conflicts of class and interest, and clashes in ideology" my book is "somewhat muted" (*JBL* 97 [1978] 299). He is quite right on the necessity of probing the politics of paradox and the social anthropology of comedy and fantasy, of role reversals and inverted stereotypes. My own book (35–37), in discussing the work of Victor Turner, deliberately pointed towards such anthropological and sociological implications but, because of my own particular concerns, these remained, as Elliott rightly observed, "somewhat muted."

My own understanding of Jesus' constant paradoxicality in word and deed is, as just noted, to see it as the almost inevitable result of his Jewish tradition turning its aniconic faith onto language itself and thus onto law and prophecy, wisdom and apocalypse. An aphorism such as the last being first and the first last was, for Jesus, a linguistic expression of the Kingdom of God, a paradoxical expression of the relationship between the divine and the human. But such paradoxical aphorisms and narratives could also be heard by those whose understanding was far more political than religious, by someone, for example, who might decide that Jewish peasants were "the last" and Roman occupiers "the first" and consider the saying an invitation to holy war. The Jesus tradition, in other words, may well have been remembered by many who heard it literally and read it politically within either spiritual or material, national or international parameters. Gerd Theissen has recently pointed towards such a sociology of the transmission of the Jesus materials. But one recognizes, from this safe distance, both the instability and the validity of any such interpretation. Should the revolutionary succeed, should the last become first, then, the same aphorism that undergirded the rise must now undergird the fall. Such paradoxes both generate and undermine all the applications and interpretations that can be suggested. Unless the paradox is exhausted by one such political or historical reading, it will stay to sap the success it has created and to destroy the fortress it has just helped to construct.

The politics of paradox and the sociology of comic reversal are inherently unstable processes and nowhere has that been better exemplified than in the recent book, *The Reversible World,* edited by Barbara A. Babcock. The articles in this fascinating volume examine symbolic inversion and paradoxical reversal both in image and action and in situations as disparate as the peyote hunt of the Huichol Indians of north-central Mexico and the European broadsheets (proto-comics) of the sixteenth to the nineteenth centuries. The dominant message of these studies is that all such paradoxical role-reversals and image inversions, which earlier social anthropologists tended to read as safety valves to protect and confirm social stereotypes and political fixtures, serve just as much and as often to undermine and subvert them. This instability whereby a paradox (the master serving the servants) can be read in a reactionary (how stupid!) or a conservative (only in fantasy!) or a revolutionary manner (now!) is the most striking conclusion from the volume. It is shown best in this summary statement from one of the articles (235):

> Recent studies especially have shown how reversals can be used to make statements about the social order—to affirm it, attack it, suspend it, redefine it, oppose it, buttress it, emphasize one part at the cost of another, and so forth. We see a magnificently fruitful image put to diverse purposes, capable of an overwhelming range of expression. Obviously there is no question of looking for the true or correct meaning in the use of reversals. We are dealing with a symbolic referent that has new meanings in every new context and within a single context embraces multiple and contradictory meanings simultaneously.

What could one conclude from all this concerning the paradoxicality of Jesus' religious language? From the very beginning, for example, his aphorisms and stories could be read in an apocalyptic (Q) or a gnostic (Gospel of Thomas) interpretation, and, ever since, they have notoriously mirrored the mind that read them. But this polyvalence is explained by the hard core of paradox in Jesus' own message. Such paradoxicality both generates and undermines successive interpretations and applications just as it both generates and undermines moral imperatives, ecclesiastical structures, and political programs.

And all of this connects with Ricoeur's comments in *Semeia* 4 (1975:126–27) on the relationship between religion and politics, between religious language and political language. He argued there that

> political discourse therefore is no less oriented, disoriented, and reoriented than any other form of discourse; and the specific way in which it is disoriented and reoriented is that it becomes the place of the insertion of an impossible demand, a demand that we can validly interpret in utopian terms, meaning by this a quest that cannot be exhausted by any program of action. Paradox then does not strike *praxis* any less than it does *theoria,* political *praxis* any less than the *praxis* of private morality.

(c) *Paradox and ambiguity.* But apart from Jesus' paradoxicality and its specific function within his own tradition, and apart even from how it could be read politically as well as religiously, there is the wider and more philosophical question about paradox itself. What, for example, is the difference between the paradoxes of nihilism and of mysticism? Is there both a human and an inhuman paradoxicality?

I have tried to discuss this question, in that recent book for Semeia Supplements mentioned earlier, in terms of Gershom Scholem's magnificent volume on Sabbatai Sevi in the seventeenth century. What is the difference between the paradox of the crucified Messiah in Christianity and the paradox of the apostate Messiah in Sabbatianism?

Another way of noting this same question is to recall the courage shown by the philosopher Miguel de Unamuno in the first autumn of the Spanish Civil War. Franco's rebellion was headquartered at Salamanca, of whose ancient and famous university the Basque philosopher was then rector. On October 12, 1936, Unamuno was presiding over a politico-religious celebration of the Festival of the Race in the ceremonial hall of the university. During an address by General José Millán Astray, commander of the Spanish Foreign Legion, "a man at the back of the hall cried Millán Astray's motto: '¡Viva la Muerte!' 'Long live death!' " With a hushed hall waiting in fearful anticipation, Unamuno rose to speak. "I, who have spent my life shaping paradoxes which have aroused the uncomprehending anger of others, I must tell you, as an expert authority, that this outlandish paradox is repellent to me" (Thomas: 502).

There is a difference, then, between "Who loses life saves it, who saves life loses it," on the one hand, and "Long live death," on the other. Maybe the difference is best illustrated by the fact that Unamuno, fired from his post at the university and placed under immediate house arrest, "died broken-hearted on the last day of 1936." General Millán Astray, however, lived for another twenty years.

Two

SOWER AND SEED

In the name of Annah the Allmaziful, the Everliving,
the Bringer of Plurabilities, haloed be her eve, her
singtime sung, her rill be run, unhemmed as it is un-
even!

(Joyce: 104)

Avery recent and very interesting article on Jesus' parable of The Sower begins by noting that, "despite numer-
ous exegetical-hermeneutical probings of the Parable of
the Sower, the scholarly community is far from reaching
consensus on what message Jesus intended to convey
through the Parable. Some commentators concede his
message is lost to us. Others contend it is yet to be discovered" (Weeden: 98). As a statement concerning biblical
scholarship this judgment is quite correct but the disagreement it records may also indicate that more prelimi-
nary research into our own hermeneutical presuppositions
is precisely what is needed to prepare for a solution. Compare, for example, this equally recent comment by
Wolfgang Iser. "It would not be unfair to say that, at least
since the advent of 'modern art,' the referential reduction
of fictional texts to a single 'hidden' meaning represents a
phase of interpretation that belongs to the past. This is
becoming increasingly obvious in present day literary criticism; titles such as *Against Interpretation* or *Validity in*

Interpretation show that both the attackers and the apologists realize that the techniques of interpretation can no longer be practiced without due consideration of the presuppositions underlying them" (Iser: 10).

My purpose here is to raise this question of hermeneutical presuppositions since it is a necessary preamble to any consideration of the hermeneutical task. This will be done by exploring the problem of univalence and polyvalence, unicity and plurality in interpretation, and by focusing the discussion on Jesus' parable of The Sower. This parable is peculiarly appropriate for my purpose since it is a parable about the process of parabling, a metaphor for its own hermeneutical task, a narrative of its own interpretative destiny.

Parables, one could say, are made of glass. Some parables are the glass of windows through whose clarity we see a world outside, a world framed by them for our directed vision. But others are the glass of mirrors. They consistently resist our attempts to turn them into windows and their reflective opacity reveals instead the faces of those who look upon them. But this is very far from a redundant narcissism. For these latter parables, or better *metaparables,* must, like mirrors, show us not just our faces but our eyes, not just ourselves but ourselves looking, not just what we perceive but how we perceive. If parables show us the lineaments of world, metaparables show us the foundations of world, they reveal not just the product but the process of interpretation.

1. PARABLE AND TRADITION

When one is primarily interested in the historical Jesus it is customary to isolate his original parable from the developments it received in both traditional and redactional transmission. Those later developments can thereafter be ignored. In the present case it will be necessary both to isolate this original parable and also to note how such developments reveal the hermeneutical process engendered by the parable itself.

1.1 The Present Versions

Four versions of the parable of The Sower are presently available: Matthew 13:3b–8; Mark 4:3–8; Luke 8:5–8a; Gospel of Thomas 9 (Guillaumont: 7; Robinson: 119). It will be necessary to work backwards from and through these four accounts to establish the parable told by the historical Jesus. And the major drive is not, of course, for his *ipsissima verba* but for what one might term the *ipsissima structura* of that original story.

Since the more general Two Source hypothesis of Synoptic relationships is receiving careful and detailed criticism at the present time both for the gospels in general (for example, Walker) and also for the interpretation section of this parable in particular (Wenham), and since the independence or dependence of the Thomistic and Synoptic gospels is even more heavily debated (Crossan, 1973a:244), it seems wisest to develop my analysis without any presuppositions about the relationships between these four texts of the parable. As the analysis proceeds I can then indicate which source explanation seems most correct in at least this particular case.

The parable may be broken down into the following basic units:

	Matthew	Mark	Luke	Thomas
The Sowing	13:3b–4a	4:3–4a	8:5a	9a
The Path	13:4b	4:4b	8:5b	9b
The Rocks	13:5–6	4:5–6	8:6	9c
The Thorns	13:7	4:7	8:7	9d
The Good Soil	13:8	4:8	8:8a	9e

These units may serve as sections for analysis in the following pages.

1.11 *The Sowing*

Matt 13:3b–4a: A sower went out to sow. And as he sowed . . .
Mark 4:3–4a: Listen! A sower went out to sow. And as he
    sowed . . .
Luke 8:5a: A sower went out to sow his seed; and as he
    sowed . . .
Gos. Thom. 9a: See, the sower went out, he filled his hand, he
    threw (Guillaumont); Now the sower went out, took a
    handful (of seeds), and scattered them (Robinson).

In comparing the four versions of this first unit two points are worth noting.

First, there is the specific opening words of the parable. Mark has "Listen! See," although this latter term is left untranslated above. Matthew has only "See," also left untranslated above. Luke has neither term. But Thomas has again the latter one alone, translated as either "See" or "Now." Weeden has argued, persuasively, that, "given the penchant which the creators of the Interpretation have for the word 'hear' (4:15, 16, 18, 20), and given their strong theological interest in the receptiveness or lack of receptiveness of 'hearing' the kerygma, it follows logically that the creators of the Interpretation framed the parable with 'Listen!' and 'He who has ears to hear, let him hear' " (104–106). If one held for Matthean priority here one would have to maintain that Mark himself added in the term "Listen!" in 4:3a. If one holds for Markan priority here, then the term "See" is original, the addition of "Listen!" is pre-Markan, and the discrepancy and tautology of the double admonition is retained by Mark, and solved by the elimination of the former term in Matthew and by the elimination of both terms in Luke. But it should be noted that both Matthew/Mark and Thomas have this initial "See."

Second, there is a certain paratactic and triadic structure to Thomas which is not present in the Synoptics. The verbs are either: went/filled/threw (Guillaumont) or went/took/scattered (Robinson). What the Synoptics have is three derivatives of the same root (sow) in Matthew and Mark and four of the same root in Luke.

1.12 The Path

Matt 13:4b: some seed fell along the path, and the birds came and devoured them.
Mark 4:4b: some seed fell along the path, and the birds came and devoured it.
Luke 8:5b: some seed fell along the path, and was trodden under foot, and the birds devoured it.
Gos. Thom. 9b: Some (seeds) (men) fell on the road; the birds came, they gathered them (Guillaumont); Some fell on the road; the birds came and gathered them up (Robinson).

I shall leave aside for here questions involving the relationship of sowing and ploughing at the time of Jesus since that subject seems to be exhausted (Crossan, 1973a:245; Payne). Apart from that problem, one is immediately struck by the almost complete unanimity on this unit across the four texts. They all even have a *men* at the beginning. The only divergence is Luke's "was trodden under foot." It has been suggested that this is his own addition and that seems most likely (Carlston: 73). But in this case all the texts evince a certain paratactic and triadic structure: fell/came/gathered or devoured. And even Luke's addition does not break this pattern: fell/trodden/devoured.

1.13 *The Rocks*

Matt 13:5–6: Other seeds fell on rocky ground, where they had not much soil, and immediately they sprang up, since they had no depth of soil, but when the sun rose they were scorched; and since they had no root they withered away.

Mark 4:5–6: Other seed fell on rocky ground, where it had not much soil, and immediately it sprang up, since it had no depth of soil; and when the sun rose it was scorched, and since it had no root it withered away.

Luke 8:6: And some fell on the rock; and as it grew up, it withered away, because it had no moisture.

Gos. Thom. 9c: Others fell on the rock (*petra*) and did not strike root in the earth and did not produce ears (Guillaumont); Others fell on rock, did not take root in the soil, and did not produce ears (Robinson).

This unit is as striking as the preceding one, but for opposite reasons. First, there are more major differences between the versions in this case than in any other unit of the parable. Second, the rocks section in Mark, for example, is about twice as long as the path or thorns section (33 words against 13 and 17 respectively, in Greek), and is about half again as long as the good soil section (33 words against 24 words, in Greek). With attention thus drawn forcibly to this unit, one notices that there are two major differences between the four versions to be considered.

First, there is the phrase "where it had not much soil" which is present in Matthew/Mark but absent in Luke and Thomas. The phrase is somewhat redundant as a gloss on the terms "rocky ground" and, especially in the light of the two following repetitions of the same idea in Matthew and Mark ("since they/it had no depth of soil" and "since they/ it had no root"), it is probably best considered, as Weeden does (105), as an addition. Since Matthew and Mark have the addition and Luke and Thomas lack it, this raises the question whether these latter versions have simply removed an obvious redundancy or represent an earlier and independent tradition of the Matthew/Mark one. This question will have to be postponed until after consideration of the second major difference between the four versions of the rocky ground section.

Second, then, there is the problem that both Matthew and Mark have a certain conflict of imagery between the slow withering and instant scorching, between seed which grows up from shallow soil and eventually withers away and seed which is scorched by the first day's burning sun. The division is as follows:

slow withering (no root):	13:5, 6b	4:5, 6b
immediate scorching (sun):	13:6a	4:6a

Once again, there is no such discrepancy in Luke and Thomas, neither of which have any mention of the sun's immediate scorching. This is an extremely important question and I have already had to discuss it in two other places (Crossan, 1973a:244–51, 1973b:39–44). It will be necessary to refer to those earlier conclusions here and to discuss them in terms of Weeden's recent article on the same subject (Weeden: 98–101).

It is possible, of course, to reconcile the divergent images of gradual withering and immediate scorching by considering this latter as "graphic narrative style, which is not concerned with the passage of time" (Linnemann: 116). Still, in view of the sun's absence from Luke and Thomas as well as the other problems of undue length and triple redundancy ("not much soil . . . no depth of soil . . . no root"), it seems much better to discuss the possibilities of expansion (Weeden: 99) and to do so in some detail.

(a) *Mark 4:5–6.* For reasons which will become clear later on I intend to begin with a consideration of the Markan version. If the problems of length, redundancy, and imagery in Mark 4:5–6 derive from expansion, what is original, traditional, and redactional in these verses?

My first answer to that question had proposed that the pre-Markan content was "Other seed fell on rocky ground and when the sun rose it was scorched" (4:5a, 6a) and that "this was expanded by the addition of the sections in vss. 5b, 6b which thereby created the problems of length, redundancy, and divergent images" (Crossan, 1973a:246). In preparing the article containing that opinion for inclusion in a later book I became convinced that, while the triple problem was real, my proposed solution was quite incorrect. I therefore proposed a different solution, namely, that the slow withering was pre-Markan and the immediate scorching by the sun was Mark's redactional expansion (Crossan, 1973b:40–41). Although Weeden (98–101) has argued that my *former* solution was correct, I am still very much convinced that it was not and that it was necessary to change it to that *later* one. The reasons for the change are both internal and external to Mark's gospel. The two internal ones are by far the more important and these will be given immediately. The external ones will appear in discussing Luke and Thomas on this section.

First, with regard to *form*. Markan redactional technique and compositional style are evidenced by this expansion. Recent Markan studies have established that this author very frequently indicates he is inserting something into a source by framing it with exactly the same phrase before and after it (Donahue: 77–84; Kee: 54–56). One rather obvious example is his repetition of "Rise, take up your pallet" before (2:9) and after (2:11) his redactional insertion concerning the Son of Man's power on earth to forgive sins (2:10). In the case of the rocky soil in 4:5–6 the phrase "since it had no" appears both before (4:5b) and after (4:6b) the unit concerning the sun: "and when the sun rose it was scorched" (4:6a). A similar instance of Markan redactional technique appears in the last of his parables in this chapter. In The Mustard Seed the phrase "when sown" appears before (4:31a) and after (4:32a) the Markan insertion on "the smallest of all seeds on earth" in 4:31b (Crossan, 1973b:46). From this I would conclude that it was Mark himself who inserted the sun's scorching (4:6a) and duplicated the frames "since it had no" (4:5b, 6b).

Second, this internal argument from Markan *form* is confirmed by an equally internal one from Markan *content*. What Markan theme motivated this insertion concerning the scorching sun? This may be clarified by placing 4:5–6 in parallel columns with its interpretation in Mark 4:16–17:

Other seed fell on rocky ground,	And these in like manner are the ones sown upon rocky ground,
where it had not much soil,	
	who, when they hear the word, immediately receive it with joy;
and immediately it sprang up, *since it had no depth* of soil; and when the sun rose it was scorched, and *since it had no* root it withered away.	and they have no root in themselves, but endure for a while; then when tribulation or persecution arises on account of the word, immediately they fall away.

The Markan addition of the scorching sun in 4:6a corresponds to the equally Markan addition of "tribulation or persecution" in 4:17b. Mark needs scorching sun and not just slow withering in the parable because he intends tribulation and persecution in the interpretation. And persecution is a very Markan theme. Recall, for example, the presence of "with persecutions" in 10:30 (compared with Matt 19:29 and Luke 18:30) and the "tribulation" in 13:19, 24. I would underline that I am not suggesting that Mark added 4:6a (sun) to align this verse better with a pre-Markan 4:17a (tribulation and persecution) but rather that Mark added *both* 4:6a and 4:17b to his pre-Markan source which had lacked both.

Although certainty is hardly an appropriate word in such delicate and tentative literary analysis, it seems to me to be as secure a conclusion as is possible in such matters to maintain that Mark himself had expanded 4:5–6 as just described.

If, as argued earlier, "where it had not much soil" (4:5a) is an addition, and if, as has just been argued, the mention of the sun (4:6a) with its redactionally repeated frames of "since it had no depth of soil" and "since it had no root" is a Markan addition, it seems most likely that the former addition was not effected by Mark but derives from the pre-Markan tradition (so Weeden: 105). This can all be summarized as follows:

Antepenultimate Markan Text	Pre-Markan Addition	Markan Addition
Other seed fell on rocky ground,		
	where it had not much soil,	
and immediately it sprang up, *since it had no*		
		depth of soil; and when the sun rose it was scorched, and *since it had no*
root it withered away.		

This postulated antepenultimate Markan text solves the difficulties of length (about 15 words in Greek), redundancy, and imagery first noted for the Matthew/Mark unit concerning the rocks. It also presents a paratactic and triadic unit: fell/sprang up/withered (See Weeden: 100).

(b) *Matt 13:5–6.* There is also one other very important

conclusion which can be derived from the presence of *Markan* redaction in 4:5–6. Up to this point Matthew and Mark have presented remarkably homogeneous texts. The only divergence worth noting had been Mark's "Listen! See . . ." (4:3a) as against Matthew's "See . . ." (13:3b), and although this seems more easily explained by Markan priority, it *could* also be argued from Matthean priority by claiming that Mark added in the "Listen!" in line with the pre-Markan 4:9.

Now, however, only one conclusion is possible. Since Mark himself expanded 4:5–6 and since Matthew has it almost verbatim, Matthew must have used Mark as a source for this verse and presumably for the entire parable. From now on, therefore, my hypothesis will be that Matthew is using Mark as his source.

(c) *Luke 8:6.* The version in Luke is, however, a very different case. On the one hand, he has *none* of the problems of length, redundancy, imagery just seen for Mark and Matthew. But on the other hand, he does have the seed fall "on the rock" (*petra*) rather than "on the rocky ground" (*petrōdes*), and it fails there because "it had no moisture" rather than because "it had no root."

There are two major possibilities to explain this situation. First, if Luke is using Mark as his source, one could argue that this "is almost a textbook example of his general tendency to smooth out, vary, and improve Mark's somewhat rambling style" (Carlston: 70). Although, of course, Mark was not rambling but redacting 4:5–6, this would be the ordinary explanation within the Two Source theory. Second, there is the possibility that Luke has another source than Mark for this parable and, whether he also knows Mark or not, he prefers that other source at least for this verse. One would then almost automatically wonder whether other Lukan divergences from Mark and

Matthew likewise derive from this special source for the parable. Along this line of thought, it has been suggested that, at least for the interpretation of the parable, "Luke knew the pre-synoptic tradition and Mark" and that "he was working in tension with the Marcan and the pre-Marcan versions in mind" so that he "reverts later on to the version with which he was familiar, probably in the church's oral tradition" (Wenham: 318). Those then are the major options: either Luke has severely rewritten Mark or Luke has access to independent tradition.

In earlier discussions of this parable I was working within the general presuppositions of the Two Source theory and I concluded that "Luke's literary instinct pruned the story back very close to its original pre-Markan version" (Crossan, 1973b:40, see also 1973a:245–46). But if one adopts, as I am trying to do here, a stance of *initial methodological neutrality* towards *any* Synoptic source theory and tries each unit on its own merits, this case becomes much more difficult. Nevertheless, for the following reasons, I would still prefer the above conclusion although, of course, while it is *most probable* that Matthew used Mark for The Sower, it is only *just possible* that Luke did so.

The first reason concerns the earlier phrase "was trodden under foot" in Luke 8:5b alone. It has been noted that "this expansion does not seem to fit Palestinian agricultural customs or improve the picture, since birds are *less* likely to get the seed after it has been trampled than (as in Mk) before" (Carlston: 73). In other words, this phrase doubles and confuses the imagery: seed *trodden* by people and/or *eaten* by birds. This means that coming from Luke 8:5b into 8:6 we have not yet established good evidence of original tradition but rather of Lukan redactional change since "both 'tread under foot' and 'birds of the heaven'

(8:5) may be for Luke terms of eschatological destruction" (Carlston: 73).

The second reason is somewhat ambiguous. There is the phrase "on the rock" in 8:6 as against "on rocky ground" in Mark. It is possible to argue that, if the area "were simply *rock,* as Luke interprets it, the birds would have eaten this seed as well" (Carlston: 73, n.14). However, since Gos. Thom. 9c also has "rock" (in Greek) and since he understands it to mean, I take it, on rocky ground with shallow soil, and since we already argued that the pre-Markan tradition felt an explanatory gloss was necessary ("where it had not much soil") even for "on rocky ground," it may well be that "on the rock" is simply an abbreviated form of "on rocky ground" and that both translate the same type of area where, namely, "the underlying limestone, thinly covered with soil, barely shows above the surface" (Jeremias: 12). Hence, this fact can be used just as well for original tradition as for redactional activity in Luke 8:6.

A third reason against Luke's account as independent tradition is much more significant. Both the pre-Markan ("since it had no root") and the Thomistic ("did not take root") versions mention the lack of *roots,* presumably because the soil was so shallow. Luke notes only the lack of *moisture,* yet all the moisture in the world is of little assistance if the soil is too shallow for rooting. Lack of roots and not lack of moisture is the problem with rocky ground.

Finally, there is the question of Luke's interpretation of his 8:6 in 8:13. I have already proposed that Mark himself added the "sun" in 4:5–6 and also its corresponding "tribulation or persecution" in 4:17b. Luke has no "sun" in his parable at 8:6 but his corresponding interpretation does include a redacted version of Mark 4:17b in Luke 8:13:

and they have no root in themselves, but endure for a while (*proskairoi*);	but these have no root, they believe for a while (*pros kairon*)
then, when tribulation or persecution arises on account of the word, immediately they fall away (4:17b)	and in time of temptation fall away (8:13)

Thus Luke's "temptation" has replaced Mark's "tribulation or persecution." And, of course, the scorching sun is a better image for the latter than the former phenomenon. Because of this it seems better to conclude that Luke, like Matthew, is using Mark for this parable and its interpretation, and that he changed Mark 4:5–6 in his 8:6 and Mark 4:17b in his 8:13 not only because of general stylistic reasons but specifically to remove the scorching sun as a metaphor for persecution since persecution was to be changed into temptation in his own interpretation of the parable.

(d) *Gos. Thom.* 9c. The Thomistic version has been touched on in considering the Lukan text and requires only two additional comments.

First, it is every bit as good as the antepenultimate one postulated earlier before pre-Markan and Markan additions. Both speak of lack of roots resulting from too shallow soil over a rocky base. Second, and once again, both the antepenultimate Markan and the Thomistic texts are paratactic and triadic: fell/sprang up/withered (Mark), and fell/take root/not produce (Thomas).

1.14 *The Thorns*

Matt 13:7: Other seeds fell upon thorns, and the thorns grew up and choked them.

Mark 4:7: Other seed fell among thorns and the thorns grew up and choked it, and it yielded no grain.

Luke 8:7: And some fell among thorns; and the thorns grew with it and choked it.

Gos. Thom. 9d: And others fell on the thorns; they choked the seed and the worm ate them (Guillaumont); And others fell on thorns; they choked the seed(s) and worms ate them (Robinson).

Apart from the phrase "and it yielded no grain" present only in Mark and the statement that "the worms ate them" only in Thomas, the versions are rather unanimous.

In my earlier discussion of that phrase in Mark I noted that it is disruptive of the triadic pattern (fell/grew up/choked/yielded) which had been appearing steadily throughout the reconstructed parable. My suggestion was that the phrase "refers immediately to the seed among thorns but also reflects back on all the wasted seed in 4:3–7" (Crossan, 1973b:41, 1973a:249). But both Weeden (103) and Carlston (70) see in it an influence from the interpretation in 4:19 ("it proves unfruitful") back into the parable itself, and this seems a better explanation. I would also agree with Weeden that this anticlimactic insert, wisely omitted by both Matthew and Luke in using Mark as a source, was present in the pre-Markan tradition and derives from those who added the interpretation to the parable and composed the parabolic complex used by Mark in this chapter.

That leaves only "the worms" in Thomas. It is very difficult to decide between antepenultimate Mark and Thomas on this point. In favor of its originality is its earthiness but against it is the repetitiveness of the birds on the path and the worms among the thorns both eating the seed. It also breaks a certain triadic appropriateness in having the three realms of the natural world, the animal, mineral, and vegetable, represented by the birds, rocks, and thorns respectively. So, but very tentatively, I would prefer antepenultimate Mark over Thomas here. But, even with changed content, both the antepenultimate Markan text (fell/grew up/choked) and the Thomistic one (fell/choked/ate) are, once again, both paratactic and triadic.

1.15 The Good Soil

Matt 13:8: Other seeds fell on good soil and brought forth grain, some a hundredfold, some sixty, some thirty.

Mark 4:8: And other seeds fell into good soil and brought forth grain, growing up and increasing and yielding thirtyfold and sixtyfold and a hundredfold.

Luke 8:8a: And some fell into good soil and grew, and yielded a hundredfold.

Gos. Thom. 9e: And others fell on the good earth; and it brought forth fruit (*karpos*); it bore sixty per measure and one hundred twenty per measure (Guillaumont); And others fell on the good soil and produced good fruit; it bore sixty per measure and a hundred and twenty per measure (Robinson).

In this terminal unit the differences and problems tend to multiply. Two easier ones may be discussed immediately. There is first of all the "growing up and increasing" which is present only in Mark. In my earlier work on this parable I suggested that this was "a strange and somewhat belated way of specifying the already noted 'brought forth grain' " (Crossan, 1973b:41, 1973a:248) and I considered it a *Markan* redactional expansion. Weeden (101, 104), however, has argued persuasively that the insertions in 4:5 ("where it had not much soil"), in 4:7 ("and it yielded no grain"), and here in 4:8 ("growing up and increasing") are *all pre-Markan* expansions.

A second problem arises from the reversal of the numbers between Matthew (100, 60, 30) and Mark (30, 60, 100). But, still following the extremely strong presumption of Matthean usage of Mark, this could easily be explained as reflecting Matthew's concerns with his community's failing zeal (Carlston: 25). There are not only the path, the rocks, and the thorns, but there are even weeds among the good seed (Matt 13:24–30). In the light of Matthew's concerns with community failures throughout his gospel, a declining rather than a rising yield is quite appropriate (Kingsbury: 60).

But the far more difficult problems in this unit concern the *yield* in the good soil. These are three in number: the measurement, the amount, and the meaning of the yield.

First, there is the measurement of the yield. What exactly is being measured here? For Jeremias it is the yield *of the whole field:* "We must not consider v. 8 as the description of a specially fruitful portion of the field, but as another point of time, namely the whole field at the moment of harvest" (150). For Linnemann it is the yield *of the individual ear:* "It is not the yield of the whole field that is meant here—this is calculated after the threshing from the proportion of seed to harvest—but the fruit produced by the individual grain. In that country each ear bears thirty-five seeds on the average, but up to sixty are often counted and occasionally even a hundred in one ear" (117). I had accepted Linnemann's view in my earlier work (Crossan, 1973a:248, n.19, 1973b:43), and I still think she is correct as against Jeremias. The main reason is that one can hardly assess the yield of the whole field *in three different ways.* A farmer could easily assess his total yield by knowing the quantity of seed sown and the final quantity of grain produced for the whole field, and Jeremias himself admits this: "Dalman's abundant statistics show that a tenfold yield acounts as a good harvest, and a yield of seven and a half as an average one" (150, n.84). And if three different yields are impossible for an entire field so also would the assessment of three different yields for three different sections of the same field be likewise impossible. A farmer would have to separate and measure three amounts of seed and then, in harvesting, separate and measure the three yields produced by that division. And that way madness lies. Hence it is far better to accept Linnemann's understanding that 30, 60, and 100 represent a triadic enumeration of the amount of grain in various ears per units of seed sown. They are obviously round numbers and in a symbolic threesome. One need hardly imagine the harvesters counting the grains in each and every ear. That way also madness lies.

But, as Linnemann realizes, her opinion applies only to the Synoptic and not to the Thomistic version. While the yield of an individual ear is assessed against the seed from which it grew, "the yield of the field is calculated from the *whole* of the seed" (including that lost or fruitless). Were it otherwise the Synoptics "would have to say: 'The field bore thirty-, sixty-, a hundredfold.' This is how the passage runs in the Gospel of Thomas" (181, n.13). Thus the Synoptics assess the yield of grain per ear while Thomas computes the yield of grain produced over total seed sown. How and why he can compute *two* yields will be discussed later.

Second, there is the question of the amount of the yield: 30, 60, 100 in Mark; 100 in Luke; 60, 120 in Thomas. Leaving aside the problem of how the yield is being assessed, which of these three enumerations seems to be the more original? Throughout my analysis both here and earlier (Crossan, 1973a:249) I have underlined the triadic structure of each unit both in the antepenultimate Markan text and in the Thomistic one as well. This can be summarized by noting the verbs involved:

Antepenultimate Markan Version	*Thomistic Version* (*Guillaumont*)
went/sow/sowed	went/filled/threw
fell/came/devoured	fell/came/gathered
fell/sprang up/withered	fell/strike/produce
fell/grew/choked	fell/choked/ate
fell/brought forth/yielding	fell/brought forth/bore

Even where there are slight differences in content between the twin versions, this triadic structure exercises a powerful hold on the narrative. You will also notice that, after the introduction concerning the sowing, the four units which detail what happened to the seed are homogeneous in content. Each mentions: (1) the *region* where the seed fell; (2) the *reception* which the seed met; (3) the *result* which the seed produced (see also Weeden: 105, 112).

Against such a repeated triadic structure there can be only one answer on the original content of the terminal unit. It had to be 30, 60, 100, with (1) a double triad in the last unit: fell/brought forth/yielding, and then 30/60/100; (2) a triadic decimal progression in 30/60; (3) climaxed not by the expected 90 or 120 but by a terminal 100. My explanation for this is as before. "The 60/120 of Thomas may be better mathematics than the 30/60/100 of Mark but it is not as good poetry. B. H. Smith has discussed the special problems of poetic closure especially for paratactic structures and concluded that 'one of the most common and substantial sources of closural effects in poetry is the terminal modification of a formal principle.' The constant use of threesomes is broken here by the terminal 100 (rather than 90 or 120) which is itself a number representing consummation or completeness. The parable is ended" (Crossan, 1973b:43–44).

If Mark's 30, 60, 100 is the most original of the

amounts, what of Luke's 100? If one had opted for independent Lukan tradition in this parable, the 100 would presumably be another proof of it. It would also be proof, I think, that his independent tradition is not too well preserved on this point. It is far easier to go from 30, 60, 100 to 100 than vice versa. It is therefore probably best to consider that Luke is simply using Mark and, disliking his plurality, has reduced it to consummate unity "since throughout Luke-Acts the inexorable advance of the Gospel in the face of obstacles is so important. But the use of the single figure shows that the greatness of the harvest is not the central theme in Luke. No figure of any kind is given in the explanation" (Carlston: 73).

Finally, what are we to make of Thomas' 60, 120, especially as total yields for the entire field? If Jeremias, after Dalman, is correct in claiming that "a tenfold yield counts as a good harvest" (150, n.84) and that "the abnormal yield of the soil in the Messianic Age is already depicted in eschatological metaphors both in the OT and in the rabbinic and pseudepigraphical literature" (150, n.86), one could explain Thomas' impossible proportions as the exaggeration of eschatological consummation and-or gnostic perfection. But since I still have no idea why one should or could compute *more than one yield* (seed sown against grain produced) for a field, I am inclined to see in Thomas' figures not so much eschatological plenitude as simple agricultural ignorance. Unless one concludes that such plenitude is portrayed not only by the magnitude of the yield (be it 60 or 120) but also by the doubling of that yield (both 60 and 120), it seems better to think that somewhere in transmission the representative triple computation by ear became a double computation by field and so became either miracle or nonsense.

Finally, there is the question of the meaning of the yield, "the notoriously obscure significance of the progression

with which the parable ends (30–60–100)" (Carlston: 139).
Jeremias and Linnemann are here, necessarily, in strict disagreement. Jeremias, reading the yield of the *whole field,*
must conclude that "the abnormal tripling, after the orien-
tal fashion, of the harvest's yield (thirty, sixty, a hundredfold) symbolizes the eschatological overflowing of the divine fullness, surpassing all human measure" (150). But,
once again, this explains only the magnitude of the yield
and not its triadic character. Linnemann, therefore, maintains that "regarded as the yield of individual ears the
figures remain entirely within the bounds of possibility and
can hardly be interpreted as signs of eschatological plenty,
particularly when one compares the fantastic figures given
in the Rabbinic parallels" (181, n.13). The triadic yield, in
other words, is as normally possible and naturally explica-
ble as is the triadic loss.

1.2 The Jesus Version

It is now possible to sum up my conclusions concerning
the earliest version of the parable discernible behind and
through our present four accounts. It will then be necessary to decide if such an earliest construct is from Jesus or
elsewhere.

First, the two best texts we have are those of Thomas (as
is) and of the antepenultimate Mark (minus both pre-
Markan and Markan additions). This would support Hel-
mut Koester's claim that, in Thomas, Jesus' teachings
"either are present in a more primitive form or are developments of a more primitive form of such sayings"
(Robinson: 117). Second, both these texts indicate a common ancestral text which was extremely paratactic
(Carlston: "Mark's 23 *kais* in the parable are reduced to 10
by both Luke and Matthew" [70]) and triadic. Third, although if one had to choose one text over the other, Mark
would have to be the one selected, the first three units

(sowing, path, rocks) are better preserved in Thomas while the last two units (thorns, good soil) are better preserved in antepenultimate Mark. Fourth, in the parable, Mark and Luke consistently see the seed as a collective singular, while Matthew and Thomas see it as a plural. It has been suggested as "probable that the plurals in the parable represent the influence of the explanation, where interest in the application has taken precedence over the story of the sowing itself" (Carlston: 24). This seems a very plausible explanation, but since Thomas has no application yet still has the plurals, it would be necessary to hold that as soon as one begins, explicitly in the Synoptics and implicitly in Thomas, to apply the parable to the responses of divergent hearers, one also tends to move the seed from collective singular to plural. Fifth, the images of *both* failure and success, of *both* losses and yields are strictly and serenely normal. On this most important point I must disagree emphatically with Weeden who claims that "one discovers not only that the final instance of sowing leads to a culminating jolt of extreme proportion and extravagant abundance, but also that each of the episodes of the wasted seed terminates in a similarly extreme manner. They end on a jarring note of extraordinary violence. The seeds are devoured, scorched, choked. It is almost as though the fate of all the seeds, not just the fate of the abundantly producing seed, should be marked with an exclamation point" (111). Apart completely from my own preference for Linnemann over Jeremias on the normalcy of the triple yield, I find this claim for extraordinary violence in the triple loss quite unconvincing. Birds and worms, rocks and thorns, and even the scorching sun (had it been original) are the normal and natural opponents of the seeds's success. They have, one might say, nothing against the seed. Surely if one required a nature red in tooth and claw one could create better images of extreme and extraordinary violence than the ones presented in this serenely pastoral parable. One need only study the apocalyptic bestiary to see some alternatives. Indeed, the parable's triadic construction, with threes emphasized by both form and content, tends also to create an impression of *repetition* and therefore of *expectation* and *normalcy*. "If we think of the trebling characteristic of the folk tale, and of all formulaic literature, we may consider that the repetition by three constitutes the minimal repetition to the perception of series, which would make it the minimal intentional structure of action, the minimum plot" (Brooks: 288). Repetition and seriality persuade us of normalcy and inevitability. Sixth, and here one finds a fairly unexpected point, "The German title of the parable, 'the field with four different kinds of soil', is misleading, and only justified by reference to the interpretation" (Linnemann: 180, n.2). The parable is about *three stages of loss and three degrees of gain.* Some seed is lost *immediately,* left by the path it does not even get under the ground. Some is lost *eventually,* it gets under the soil but, rootless, soon withers. Some gets down deep enough under the soil to grow but is *ultimately* choked by the accompanying thistles. So also some produces 30 or 60 or 100 grains per ear in good soil. Should these latter be taken simply as poetically different types or as numerically superior degrees of yield? The triad of losses, be they sooner or later, are all failures and no farmer would care much for one over the other. Here the triad is clearly symbolical of the normal multiplicity of failure-causing factors. I am therefore inclined to read the triad of yield in the same way. Any farmer would, of course, prefer 100 grains on every ear and to this extent 100 is *better* than 30 or 60 grains per ear. Still the parable's tone of agricultural normalcy would lead one to read the triple yield not as a hierarchy of perfection but as the symbolical expression of the necessarily diverse possibilities of success. If all ears

contained 100 grains, the parable would probably have
entered the realm of the extraordinary. Indeed, if all ears
contained the same number, whatever it was, the parable
would probably partake of the extraordinary. Therefore, I
would consider that the different stages of loss (immediate, eventual, ultimate) and the different degrees of
gain (30, 60, 100) do not symbolize hierarchy but simple
plurality.

It is interesting, however, that almost every commen-
tator on this parable talks about *the harvest* and thereby
smoothly obliterates this triple distinction of yield. This is
true from Dodd who speaks of the "harvest" (8), "good
harvest" (12), and even "excellent harvest" (146) to
Weeden who twice refers to the "bountiful harvest" (116).
But Carlston is acute enough to note that "technically, the
harvest is not mentioned at all—only the yield" (141). And
this yield is, normally and naturally, as diverse as is the
loss.

Seventh, and possibly this is the most striking feature of
all, while the precise methods and reasons of failure are
clearly spelled out, the precise modes of success are not
detailed in any way. We know what makes bad soil bad
(path, rocks, thorns) but what makes good soil good? Once
again Carlston has noted that the story mentions this "kind
of soil which will prevent external dangers (birds, sun,
thorns) from destroying the seed—although interestingly
enough just what is required to be this kind of soil is not
spelled out" (144).

These seven points detail the major aspects of the earliest version recoverable through and behind our present
fourfold narrative. Could such a parable stem originally
from the historical Jesus? I would argue that it could for
one general and one specific reason.

The general reason, which is really the *criterion of dissimilarity applied to form rather than content* (Crossan, 1976:

177), is based on the fact that the creative and poetic narrative parable was a pedagogical genre almost totally undeveloped by the early church itself (Johnston, 1977) and which does not seem to have been prevalent in Jewish tradition until somewhat later (Neusner, 1971, 1972:376). This leaves me with the general presupposition that any creative narrative parable in the New Testament stems from Jesus unless and until the contrary can be proved.

The specific reason is how this parable coheres with Jesus' teaching elsewhere. This point has been emphatically denied by Carlston's statement that "we have little evidence that Jesus was primarily concerned with the state of his hearer's hearts rather than the inbreaking Kingdom and its implications for all of human life. Insofar as the parable is primarily concerned with such subjective differences among men it represents an emphasis that is peripheral, if not totally foreign to Jesus' message" (146). This seems, however, to be a rather false dichotomy. Jesus' primary concern is indeed the Kingdom but I would consider it equally clear that his is a very special understanding of this eschatological Kingdom, one which is, among other things, totally anti-apocalyptic. Not anti-apocalyptic in minor details concerning signs and times but anti-apocalyptic as deriving from a radically non-apocalyptic imagination. Jesus' Kingdom is a permanent possibility and not an imminent certainty. Still, Carlston is correct in stating that The Sower seems somewhat different from many of Jesus' other parables. I would maintain, however, that this difference arises from the fact that it is not just a teaching about the Kingdom, although it is that as well, but also a teaching about teaching the Kingdom. It is not just a parable of the Kingdom, although it is that as well, but rather as metaparable, it is a parable about parables of the Kingdom. As such it tells us about the parabler himself, about the parabled Kingdom, and about the very parable itself as well.

First, about the parabler. It reveals his deliberate self-negation since the sower, mentioned only at the start of the story, immediately disappears. It would have been quite possible to leave him out completely: "at the time of sowing, some seed fell. . . ." It would also have been easy to have retained him consistently: "and some of the sower's seed fell. . . ." Instead, he is mentioned at the start and thereafter ignored. The parable is about seed and about the inevitable polyvalence of failure and success in sowing. It is not, despite Matt 13:18 and its traditional title, about The Sower. Or, if one prefers, it is about the absence and departure, the necessary self-negation of the sower.

Second, about the parabled Kingdom. I would hold that Jesus' parable, with startling and unnerving serenity, announces an eschatological advent not marked by overpowering apocalyptic victory and transcendental univocity of yield but rather by the normal inevitability of losses and gains, by the normal inevitability of the plural possibilities of both, and by the normal inevitability of our understanding far more clearly what and how to go wrong than what and how to go right. The parable proclaims, in other words, a Kingdom whose eschatology is as polyvalent as the processes consequent upon the sowing of seed. And a polyvalent Kingdom demands a polyvalent parabling.

Third, about his own parables, all the others and even this one as well. It would indeed be strange if Jesus had chosen the parable as his special genre and never reflected on the implications of that choice. This metaparable is the result of that reflection. And its narratival metaphor entraps us all. There may indeed be wrong interpretations and we can then specify the path, the rocks, the thorns.

And there will also be good interpretations, both good and plural, and even then we shall never be really certain what makes the good soil good. When, then, the tradition changed his parable internally in the transmission, or when Thomas omitted any explicit explanation and the pre-Synoptic tradition added a canonical interpretation (canonical, therefore, as process not as product), or when exegetes, ancient and modern, deliberate intention and multiply meaning, all that happens is that the polyvalence asserted for the yield is repeatedly verified (Tolbert). But, if polyvalence is a feature of both the text's transmission and the tradition's interpretation, the drive of this polyvalence is the avoidance of polyvalence, the obliteration or obviation of the yield's serene plurality, the reduction of the threefold 30, 60, 100 to the twofold 60, 120, the single 100, or the anumerical "harvest."

2. PARABLE AND POLYVALENCE

It is clear from the preceding comments that I do not find this parable any less radical than other parables such as The Prodigal Son or The Good Samaritan which concentrate on human interaction rather than on natural processes. Thus I am again in disagreement with Weeden's claim that this parable's "imaging of the Kingdom suggests that God's activity is not always existentially disruptive of the space-time continuum but is, at least on occasion, instrumental in preserving and bringing about the actualization of the purpose of the world of space and time" (114). Since I believe in any case that *analogia entis* is always but a facet of *analogia mentis,* I do not find Jesus' "natural" parables any less devastating than his "cultural" ones. That is, the distinction of "natural" and "cultural" is cultural and one's view of "nature" is always culturally or at least mentally conditioned.

2.1 The Interpretation of Parable

This analysis is confirmed for me by the way in which interpreters have sought to avoid or ignore the presence of the triadic yield from the very beginning of the parable's existence. This shows, of course, as already noted, in contemporary exegetes wishing to talk about the univocity of "harvest" rather than face the inevitable plurality of the triple yield. But, for now, I wish to focus on three moments within the first century of the parable's existence.

2.11 Parabolic Transmission

The different citations of the triadic yield are probably the most interesting divergence in the four accounts. Only Mark retains the original parable's serenely multiple image. Matthew retains it but only by reversing its order and thereby rendering its plurality pejorative. The 100 is presumably the correct and proper result while the 60 and the 30 represent declines and failures even among the good soil. Thomas reduces the triple yield to a double one and Luke concludes this process by reducing it to a single one. Nobody, save Mark who may not have noticed its implications, was willing to leave it as it was. But, in any case, if you start with seed you end with plurality, and no matter how the text was changed the narratival metaphor was intrinsically polyvalent.

2.12 Canonical Interpretation

With an almost consensus of scholarship I consider the parable's canonical interpretation, present in the Synoptic but not the Thomistic version, to come from the tradition rather than from Jesus. But what is of present interest is that, while the Synoptics are quite ready to detail the meaning of the threefold failure, there is no attempt to explain the threefold gain. Mark and Matthew simply repeat the triadic enumeration of the parable, while Luke, as usual more redactionally ruthless, eliminates any number whatsoever (Mark 4:20; Matt 13:23; Luke 8:15).

2.13 Biblical Tradition

Going outside the Synoptic and Thomistic traditions, there is a fascinating contrast between the Pauline and the Johannine response to this image of the seed.

In 1 Corinthians 3:5–11 Paul uses two metaphors, that of the *seed* and that of the *foundation*. And one can almost see him begin to realize the polyvalent implications of the seed image and veer abruptly to that of the univalent foundation. "I planted, Apollos watered, but God gave the growth. So neither he who plants nor he who waters is anything, but only God who gives the growth. He who plants and he who waters are equal, and each shall receive his wages according to his labor. For we are God's fellow workers; you are God's field, [*and now the metaphor shifts*] God's building. According to the grace of God given to me, like a skilled master builder I laid a foundation, and another man is building upon it. Let each man take care how he builds upon it. For no other foundation can any one lay than that which is laid, which is Jesus Christ." Univalent foundations are safer than polyvalent seeds.

But if Paul prefers the image of the foundation for the preaching of Christ, John is quite willing to accept the implications of the seed metaphor. In John 12:24 Jesus says, "Truly, truly, I say to you, unless a grain of wheat falls into the earth and dies, it remains alone; but if it dies, it bears much fruit" (see, especially, Forestell). Instead of the unchanging univocity of a foundation, we have the polyvalent metamorphoses of a seed. Jesus is now no longer sower but a seed.

But what is especially fascinating is that all this process, then as now, and even when it is seeking to mute the parable's polyvalence, serves only to establish it. The parable remains always a metaphor for its own hermeneutical task.

2.2 The Interpretation of Interpretation

This final section intends to raise questions rather than draw conclusions. Accepting the parable of The Sower as a parable of parabling the Kingdom, as a metaparable of hermeneutical polyvalence, as a mirror rather than a window parable, I can see certain important connections between the interpretation of interpretation it proposes and specific problems in fields as diverse as politics and education, literature, philosophy, and theology. Present space renders all these points programmatic for the future.

2.21 *Authorial Intention*

The debate over the value of authorial intention for literary criticism, exemplified in the writings of E. D. Hirsch as against Hans-Georg Gadamer (Hoy), is somewhat circumvented in this parable. Here the author proposes a polyvalent response as the normal and natural result to be expected. This is not an invitation to hermeneutical anarchy since the textual structure is a far more stringent control than any authorial intention unless, of course, the latter be identified with the former. But Wolfgang Iser (230–31) has indicated very clearly the polyvalent possibilities of structural control over the presumably univalent intentionality of authorial control.

> The aleatory rule, in contradistinction to regulative and constitutive rules, does not lay down the course to be followed, but only indicates those courses which are *not* to be followed. For the most part, it is the reader's own competence that will enable the various possibilities to be narrowed down—it is he who supplies the 'code' of the 'aleatory rule'. At the same time,

though, it is the negative determinacy of this rule that conditions the whole range of gestalten that may emerge from the same text. And if there is not *one* specific meaning of a literary text, this 'apparent deficiency' is, in fact, the productive matrix which enables the text to be meaningful in a variety of different contexts.

There probably are not too many places where Henry James and Franz Kafka find themselves in verbatim agreement. But each, in each's own way, that is, in forty-three pages for James and in a half page for Kafka, has written a parable about interpretation in which an author gives some advice on the search for authorial intention. In James' story, "The Figure in the Carpet," there is a determined search for the "intention" (281, 282) or even the "general intention" (285, 286, 296, 313) in Vereker's writings. Vereker's own advice is repeated twice: "Give it up, give it up!" (285, 289). And in Kafka's parable a stranger asks a policeman the way to the railroad station: "He smiled and said: 'From me you want to learn the way?' 'Yes,' I said, 'since I cannot find it myself.' 'Give it up, give it up,' said he, and turned away with a great sweep, like someone who wants to be alone with his laughter" (see Politzer: 1–22). These two parables are negative statements ("Give it up, give it up!") of which Jesus' story is the positive equivalent.

Thus, in a brilliant metacommentary on the interpretation of James's "The Turn of the Screw," Shoshana Felman has recently written that, for James, "the literal is 'vulgar' because it *stops* the *movement* constitutive of meaning, because it blocks and interrupts the endless process of metaphorical substitution. The vulgar, therefore, is anything which misses, or falls short of, the dimension of the symbolic, anything which rules out, or excludes, meaning as a loss and as a flight—anything which strives, in other words, to eliminate from language its inherent silence, anything which misses the specific way in which a text *actively* 'won't tell' " (107). And again, later in the same essay, accompanied by a magnificent misprint: "Far from following the incessant slippage, the unfixable movement of the signifying chaim from link to link, from signifier to signifier, the critic, like the governess, seeks to *stop* the meaning, to *arrest* signification, by a grasp, precisely of the Screw (or of the 'clue'), by a firm hold on the Master-Signifier" (191).

2.22 Totalitarian Univalence

Is a too great thirst for univalence an indication of totalitarian imagination? Or, in other words, even if univalence is not always totalitarian, must totalitarianism always be univalent? If one understands univalence to be the normal situation of human communication and polyvalence to be a confusing interruption by artists and comedians, is such an understanding totalitarian? And if, on the contrary, one accepts polyvalence as the inevitable concomitant of the arbitrariness and conventionality of the sign, does this help to preserve the freedom of human play? Will it not be vitally important to decide whether polyvalence is primordial and only care and context can attain to univalence whenever such is necessary and appropriate, for example, in traffic signals, or whether univalence is primordial and polyvalence but the perversity of the poet and the clown?

2.23 Cognitive Development

What is the relationship between the stages of cognitive development and the divergences of scholarly interpretation on a biblical or classical, ancient or contemporary narrative? Does polyvalence in a parable's interpretation structure itself according to levels of cognitive development so that the story can validly and legitimately be in-

terpreted at the various levels of mental growth with readings appropriate for each level? And, if so, would not every interpretation reveal as much about the cognitive development of the interpreter as about the story under interpretation? One might then underline how, in the parable's yield, the 60 contains the 30 and the 100 contains them both, and how one cannot get to any later stage except through and after the former ones. Some recent work would seem to indicate that the relationship between biblical (or any) interpretation and cognitive development needs much more exploration than it has received so far (Gardner and Winner; Wilcox; Berryman).

2.24 *Primal Grammatology*

I am touching here on the unjoined debate between Walter Ong and Jacques Derrida on the primacy of oral or scribal communication. Ong proposes, brilliantly, the primacy of oral communication, arguing that speech precedes writing for both the race and the child. This is however a very dangerous argument since the gurgle and the grunt came even earlier for both. Such chronological primacy may be quite true but to make much of it may well be but the old nostalgia for those dear dead dreams of dawn. It may also be ungracious to note the irony of Ong's *writing* in defence of speech and insisting three times in one *written* paragraph that the only "real words" are oral ones (233).

Derrida, on the other hand, proposes not of course the chronological but what one might term the ontological priority of scribal over oral communication. The reason is that, in writing, the absence of the writer far better reveals the gap at the heart of the sign, a gap which is often overlooked in the give and take of oral discourse but which is, of course, equally present there as well (Derrida, 1976:xxxix, xli, lxix–lxx, 7, 23, etc.).

When Jesus' parable is placed against the background of these two views, it seems to fit much better with Derrida's grammatology than with Ong's orality. The irony is now reversed. Jesus tells an oral parable and in it the teller-as-sower almost instantly disappears. Written versions of the parable seem much more appropriate to this metaphor than do oral ones. In an oral situation one could demand *the* explanation from the author. And this is exactly what the tradition said happened, but said in writing. But it may well be that the debate is not really over primacy between *oral or scribal* text as over primacy between *text (oral or written) and author.* Jesus' text negates the sower to concentrate on the seed and thus the text and its metaphoric and polyvalent destiny take precedence over the author and will hold that primacy whether it is communicated orally or scribally.

2.25 *Divine Aniconicity*

Scholars have always made much of Israel's monotheism as against the polytheism of its neighbors. I am inclined to think they should place much more emphasis on Israel's gift of *aniconic* monotheism (Crossan, 1979). Polytheism had, of course, to be iconic but monotheism could be either. But iconic monotheism would surely be the most monstrous act ever produced by the human imagination. You will recall that, in Arnold Schoenberg's magnificent opera *Moses and Aaron,* as soon as there was a divine image (the golden calf) there were immediately human victims. But *aniconic monotheism* is Israel's challenge to itself and to the world and this opens the human imagination as possibly nothing else could. Such a monotheism can only generate single paradoxical images, or double contradictory images, or multiple and polyvalent images of its God. And I would maintain that this aniconic monotheism is the ul-

timate root whence Jesus derived his parable of the absent
sower and the polyvalent seed.

Derrida has said that "the trace is the erasure of self-
hood, of one's own presence, and is constituted by the
threat or anguish of its irremediable disappearance, of the
disappearance of disappearance. An unerasable trace is not
a trace, it is a full presence, an immobile and uncorruptible
substance, a son of God, a sign of parousia and not a seed,
that is, a mortal germ" (1978:230). But what if the son of
God is a mortal seed, and that becomes the parousia?

2.26 Hermeneutical Theory

This last unit locates Jesus' parable against the
background of some recent discussions on interpretation
theory. Specifically it locates it on one side of a dichotomy
which has been appearing under different names in recent
hermeneutical writings.

First, there is the distinction between *rhetoric* and *dialec-
tic* as proposed by Stanley Fish. This is an "opposition of
two kinds of literary presentation" and Fish explains them
as follows (1972:1–2):

> A presentation is rhetorical if it satisfies the needs of its
> readers. The word 'satisfies' is meant literally here; for
> it is characteristic of a rhetorical form to mirror and
> present for approval the opinions its readers already
> hold. It follows then that the experience of such a form
> will be flattering, for it tells the reader that what he has
> always thought about the world is true and that the
> *ways* of his thinking are sufficient. This is not to say that
> in the course of a rhetorical experience one is never
> told anything unpleasant, but that whatever one is told
> can be placed and contained within the categories and
> assumptions of received systems of knowledge.
>
> A dialectical presentation, on the other hand, is dis-
> turbing, for it requires of its readers a searching and

rigorous scrutiny of everything they believe in and live by. It is didactic in a special sense; it does not preach the truth, but asks that its readers discover the truth for themselves, and this discovery is often made at the expense not only of a reader's opinions and values, but of his self-esteem. If the experience of a rhetorical form is flattering, the experience of a dialectical form is humiliating.

Thus, for example, rhetoricians often tend to live much longer than dialecticians and tend to come to more peaceful deaths. But Fish (1972:378) maintains that his distinction goes deeper than that of literary presentation and is, in fact,

> an opposition of epistemologies, one that finds its expression in two kinds of reading experiences: on one side the experience of a prose that leads the auditor or reader step-by-step, in a logical and orderly manner, to a point of certainty and clarity; and on the other, the experience of a prose that undermines certainty and moves away from clarity, complicating what had at first seemed perfectly simple, raising more problems than it solves. Within this large opposition there are, of course, distinctions to be made . . . but in general the contrast holds, between a language that builds its readers' confidence by building an argument they can follow, and a language that, by calling attention to the insufficiency of its own procedures, calls into question the sufficiency of the minds it unsettles.

His textual corpus is taken from English seventeenth-century literature but he traces his own basic distinction back to the Socrates in Plato's *Phaedrus*. Jesus' parable of The Sower is, I would consider, dialectical rather than rhetorical, and one can compare what I have said about Jesus' words as seeds with what "Socrates means when he talks in the *Phaedrus* of words as 'seeds'" (1972:8). Indeed, "in terms of the functions we usually assign to language—communication of facts, opinions, desires, and emotions—they are not words at all, but *seeds,* 'for they can transmit their seed to other natures and cause the growth of fresh words in them, providing an external existence for their seed; [they] bring their possessor to the highest degree of happiness possible to attain' " (1972:14).

That last citation from Fish of the *Phaedrus* can also serve to introduce a second set of distinctions proposed by Roland Barthes and which I consider analogous to that of Fish.

In 1970 Barthes suggested a distinction between *readerly* (*lisible*) and *writerly* (*scriptible*) texts. In explaining his distinction Barthes clearly elects the writerly text, that which makes the reader participate in the writing of the text, over the readerly, that which reduces and relegates the reader to passive and obedient consumption. The "writerly text is a perpetual present, upon which no *consequent* language (which would inevitably make it past) can be superimposed; the writerly text is *ourselves writing,* before the infinite play of the world (the world as a function) is traversed, intersected, stopped, plasticized by some singular system (Ideology, Genus, Criticism) which reduces the plurality of entrances, the opening of networks, the infinity of languages." And what of the readerly texts? "They are products (and not productions), they make up the enormous mass of our literature" (1974:5). Barthes's preference for the former over the latter text is essentially ethical (1974:4):

> Why is the writerly our value? Because the goal of literary work (of literature as work) is to make the reader no longer a consumer, but a producer of the text. Our literature is characterized by the pitiless divorce which the literary institution maintains between the producer of the text and its user, between its owner and its customer, between its author and its reader.

> This reader is thereby plunged into a kind of idleness—he is intransitive; he is, in short, *serious:* instead of functioning himself, instead of gaining access to the magic of the signifier, to the pleasure of writing, he is left with no more than the poor freedom either to accept or reject the text: reading is nothing more than a *referendum.*

A few years later, in 1973, Barthes reverted to this distinction but he now rephrased it as the difference between *text of pleasure* and *text of bliss* instead of between *readerly* and *writerly* texts (1975:14): "Text of pleasure: the text that contents, fills, grants euphoria; the text that comes from culture and does not break with it, is linked to a *comfortable* practice of reading. Text of bliss: the text that imposes a state of loss, the text that discomforts (perhaps to the point of a certain boredom), unsettles the reader's historical, cultural, psychological assumptions, the consistency of his tastes, values, memories, brings to a crisis his relation with language." And in comparing this *readerly text of pleasure* with the *writerly text of bliss* Barthes insists that there is much more between them than a "difference of degree" (20). "I believe on the contrary that pleasure and bliss are parallel forces, that they cannot meet, and that between them there is more than a struggle: an *incommunication* . . . that the text of bliss always rises out of it [history] like a scandal (an irregularity), that it is always the trace of a cut, of an assertion (and not of a flowering) . . ." (21).

This brings me to the third and final connection. If there are *rhetorical and dialectical epistemologies* (Fish) whence derive, respectively, *readerly texts of pleasure and writerly texts of bliss* (Barthes), then there must be divergent interpretations for each. That is, there must be *two interpretations of interpretation* itself.

In 1964, writing a commentary on the haunting beauty of Edmond Jabès's poetry, Jacques Derrida (1978:67) used the phrase "two interpretations of interpretation" and placed one under the aegis of the rabbi and the other under that of the poet:

> The necessity of commentary, like poetic necessity, is the very form of exiled speech. In the beginning is hermeneutics. But the *shared* necessity of exegesis, the interpretive imperative, is interpreted differently by the rabbi and the poet. The difference between the horizon of the original text and the exegetic writing makes the difference between the rabbi and the poet irreducible. Forever unable to reunite with each other, yet so close to each other, how could they ever regain the *realm?* The original opening of interpretation essentially signifies that there will always be rabbis and poets. And two interpretations of interpretation.

A few years later, in 1966, he used the same phrase again but now it is explained much more fully (1978:292):

> There are thus two interpretations of interpretation, of structure, of sign, of play. The one seeks to decipher, dreams of deciphering a truth or an origin which escapes play and the order of the sign, and which lives the necessity of interpretation as an exile. The other, which is no longer turned toward the origin, affirms play and tries to pass beyond man and humanism, the name of man being the name of that being who, throughout the history of metaphysics or of ontotheology—in other words, throughout his entire history—has dreamed of full presence, the reassuring foundation, the origin and the end of play.

And in discussing this distinction Derrida is quite conscious of the difficulty of even formulating it intelligently (1978:93):

For my part, although these two interpretations must acknowledge and accentuate their difference and define their irreducibility, I do not believe that today there is any question of *choosing*—in the first place because here we are in a region (let us say, provisionally, a region of historicity) where the category of choice seems particularly trivial; and in the second, because we must first try to conceive of the common ground, and the *différance* of this irreducible difference. Here there is a kind of question, let us still call it historical, whose *conception, formation, gestation,* and *labor* we are only catching a glimpse of today. I employ these words, I admit, with a glance toward the operations of childbearing—but also with a glance toward those who, in a society from which I do not exclude myself, turn their eyes away when faced by the as yet unnamable which is proclaiming itself and which can do so, as is necessary whenever a birth is in the offing, only under the species of the nonspecies, in the formless, mute, infant, and terrifying form of monstrosity.

Within the vocabulary of these contemporary hermeneutical theories, then, Jesus' parable of The Sower is a dialectical rather than a rhetorical text, a writerly text of bliss rather than a readerly text of pleasure, and instead of our interpreting the parable we find its polyvalence has turned on us and forced us to rethink our interpretation of interpretation itself. Or, to end as I began, with *Finnegans Wake,* one could say that this Galilean sower "was at his best a onestone parable, a rude breathing on the void of to be, a venter hearing his own brauchspeech in backwards, or, more strictly, but tristurned initials, the cluekey to a worldroom beyond the roomworld" (Joyce: 100).

Three

POLYVALENCE AND PLAY

During a counterpoint class at U.C.L.A., Schoenberg
sent everybody to the blackboard. We were to solve a
particular problem he had given and to turn around
when finished so that he could check on the correct-
ness of the solution. I did as directed. He said, "That's
good. Now find another solution." I did. He said,
"Another." Again I found one. Again he said,
"Another." And so on. Finally, I said, "There are no
more solutions." He said, "What is the principle underlying all of the solutions?"

(Cage: 93)

1. METAMODEL AND PLAY

When one attempts to take parabolic polyvalence seriously, it becomes immediately necessary to attempt some
theoretical grounding for the phenomenon. How and why
is it possible to have such different exegeses of The Sower
as are evidenced from the very transmission of its text as
well as from the tradition of its interpretation? What does
this multiplicity tell us about ourselves as speakers and
hearers, as writers and readers?

In attempting a theory for this phenomenon I am fully
aware of the imperialist arrogance of such endeavors and
yet I see no alternative if one is to proceed with some
sophisticated self-criticism in reading the texts that are
one's concern.

Three notes on my method of proceeding. First, I am planning to sketch a rather large theory in a rather small space so I shall use frequent quotations to works which must serve as its wider supports. Second, I shall offer few specific examples or applications and must ask indulgence to postpone such validations for elsewhere. Third, I find it radiantly silly to think about language without having read a lot of poetry or to write about language without indicating what such reading has taught one. In honor of this prejudice, and lest I get lost on the way, I shall keep as my guide a catena of epigraphs from the American poet, A. R. Ammons.

1.1 Metamodel

> I allow myself eddies of meaning:
> yield to a direction of significance
> running
> like a stream through the geography of my work:
> you can find
> in my sayings
> swerves of action
> like the inlet's cutting edge:
> there are dunes of motion
> organizations of grass, white sandy paths of remembrance
> in the overall wandering of mirroring mind:
>
> but Overall is beyond me; is the sum of these events
> I cannot draw, the ledger I cannot keep, the accounting
> beyond the account
>
> _A. R. Ammons (1965a:5–6)_

If The Sower is a parable about parables of the Kingdom, a parable of parabling the Kingdom, and is thus a metaparable, what is the basic model or, indeed, the metamodel for this multiplicity, this presumably open-ended fecundity of actual and potential models for interpretation? In posing the question I have chosen the term *metamodel* in order to avoid the barbarism of metametaphor or the neologism of metataphor but the meaning would be the same had I asked: What is the metaphor of metaphors?

In raising this question I am attempting to rethink the theory of metaphor which I proposed in an earlier work (Crossan, 1973b). Although I was ready there to call literal language "a contradiction in terms" and figurative (metaphorical) language a "redundancy" (15), and was seeking an understanding of metaphor under the rubric of "participation" (12–15), I was still within the framework of a primarily romanticist view of language. The present attempt seeks to move this more resolutely into a structuralist viewpoint.

1.11 *Reality as Worlds*

At another time the question of metamodel or megametaphor would have seemed at best self-indulgent and at worst decadent, a vulgar play with words, a cheap paradox to catch the ears of the groundlings. One might easily have responded that over against the metaphorical stood the literal and that there was no such thing as a metaphor for metaphor since reality firmly limited metaphor and stopped immediately this dangerous and vertiginous possibility of a *regressus ad infinitum*. As long as one was convinced that the world, or reality, or whatever large and beautiful abstraction one preferred, existed out there and could be discussed independently of our perception and our understanding of it, there was no real danger that the problem of metamodel might arise with any compelling seriousness. But my basic presupposition in this chapter is that this security is lost to me and many others forever. I have argued this position elsewhere (Crossan, 1975:13–46) and will do no more than cite two philosophical statements as its present support.

Maurice Merleau-Ponty (16) has said that

> perception is thus paradoxical. The perceived thing it-
> self is paradoxical; it exists only in so far as someone
> can perceive it. I cannot even for an instant imagine an
> object in itself. As Berkeley said, if I attempt to imag-
> ine some place in the world which has never been seen,
> the very fact that I imagine it makes me present at that
> place. I thus cannot conceive a perceptible place in
> which I am not myself present.

And just as place is not outside the perceiver's perception,
so neither is world, or reality, as the sum total of worlds.
Thus John Mepham (125–126): "Different societies, cul-
tures, and languages construct different worlds. In perception we are not acquainted with 'the world itself' but with
the world as a semantic field, an endless series of 'messages', a world which is in its general forms familiar to me
by virtue of the fact that both I and it are the products of
the same culture." This means that we can no longer imagine ourselves at play with models and metaphors within
some clearing in the forest of reality whose solid trees and
firm branches establish both our security and our limitation. We have reached the point where, as Wallace Stevens
said, the shocked realist first sees reality, or, possibly better, where the shocked perceiver first sees perception.

1.12 A Metaphor of Metaphor

The first two articles of the *New Literary History* volume
"On Metaphor" raise very forcibly this question of "a
metaphor of metaphor" (Derrida, 1974:64) or "metaphors
for metaphor" (Sparshott: 85). Sparshott's question (78)
connects directly with the two philosophical quotations
just given. "If we were right in saying that one can only
think of a thing by thinking of it as something, how are we
to think of it in the initial phase when we are still mak-

ing up our minds what to think of it as?" When "as if"
(Vaihinger) expands to fill the world it has already created
the question of a/the metamodel or a/the megametaphor
must be faced and faced in full awareness of the paradoxical aspects of the endeavor. Jacques Derrida (1974:18) has
summed up this paradox most succinctly:

> Instead of venturing here on prolegomena to some fu-
> ture metaphorics, let us rather attempt to recognize the
> *conditions which make it in principle impossible* to carry
> out such a project. . . . If we wanted to conceive and
> classify all the metaphorical possibilities of philosophy,
> there would always be at least one metaphor which
> would be excluded and remain outside the system; that
> one, at least, which was needed to construct the con-
> cept of metaphor, or, to cut the argument short, the
> metaphor of metaphor.

It would be very imprudent to ignore this paradox which
haunts, or possibly fecundates, the search for a hermeneutical metamodel, a megametaphor which not only allows
but even demands the exegetical diversity seen in the preceding chapter of this book.

1.13 Gödel's Proof

What has actually appeared in Derrida's Paradox is the
incompleteness theory of Kurt Gödel. Here are three
summaries of the thesis known as Gödel's Proof. From
Nagel and Newman (6): "He proved that it is impossible
to establish the internal logical consistency of a very large
class of deductive systems—elementary arithmetic, for
example, unless one adopts principles of reasoning so
complex that their internal consistency is as open to doubt
as that of the systems themselves." From Haskell Curry
(11): "The consistency of a sufficiently powerful theory
could not be established by means which could be for-
malized in the theory itself." And from Robert Chumbley

(16): "A theory is either inconsistent or incapable of showing its own consistency." And if we accept this contention
that deductive systems cannot be both self-confirmatory
and self-consistent, we are hearing again the laughter of
Bertrand Russell as summed up by Anthony Wilden (117):
"The central thesis depends upon Russell's theory of logical types, according to which there is a discontinuity between a class and its members. The class cannot be a
member of itself, nor can one of the members *be* the class,
because the term used for the class is of a different level of
abstraction or logical type from the terms used for the
members of the class." All of which was presumably im-
plicit in Derrida's original proposal "to attempt to recog-
nize the *conditions which make it in principle impossible*" to
establish "the metaphor of metaphor."

1.14 *The Permanence of Paradox*

Since I have every intention of proceeding deeply into
this impossibility, I acknowledge immediately a double
discipline on the project. First, I shall be looking for a
metamodel which is of a higher logical type than other
possible ones so that it can subsume them while not being
itself subsumed by any of them. Second, I shall expect that
the inaugural paradox noted by Derrida, which I accept as
a destiny to be enjoyed rather than as a difficulty to be
avoided, will reappear in the metamodel itself and will be
always present at the heart or the horizon of the entire
proceedings. For, as Gregory Bateson (189) has noted,
Russell's rule both states and violates its own assertion: "It
is interesting to note that Russell's rule cannot be stated
without breaking the rule. Russell insists that all items of
inappropriate logical type be excluded (i.e., by an imaginary line) from the background of any class, i.e., he insists
upon the drawing of an imaginary line of precisely the sort
which he prohibits." Since I have already made the rather

fateful decision that there are *only* deductive systems, and that induction is simply and always a sub-system of such deduction, I am ready to accept Gödel's proof as dictating the permanence of paradox at the heart of the human. And the fundamental one which generates all the others is presumably *the paradox that, if perception creates reality, then perception (mine, yours, ours together) must also be creating the perceiver (me, you, us together).*

In all this discussion we can feel the steady pull of our inherited metaphysics. Jacques Derrida (1970:251) has noted that

> it was within concepts inherited from metaphysics that Nietzsche, Freud, and Heidegger worked, for example. Since these concepts are not elements or atoms and since they are taken from a syntax and a system, every particular borrowing drags along with it the whole of metaphysics. This is what allows these destroyers to destroy each other reciprocally—for example, Heidegger considering Nietzsche, with as much lucidity and rigor as bad faith and misconstruction, as the last metaphysician, the last 'Platonist.' One could do the same for Heidegger himself, for Freud, or for a number of others. And today no exercise is more widespread.

The result is that I must agree when Merleau-Ponty speaks of "the primacy of perception," but I must also agree when Derrida (1970:272) concludes that "whatever strikes at the metaphysics of which I have spoken strikes also at the very concept of perception. I don't believe that there is any perception." The core *paradox of the perceived perceiver,* is, once again, a destiny to be accepted not a difficulty to be solved.

1.15 Nausea in the Labyrinth

Before proceeding I would like to distinguish this structuralist basis from any existentialist parallel. I consider existentialism to be the end of one era and structuralism to be the start of another. And I consider existentialist nausea to be the ontological disappointment of one who, having been taught that there is some overarching logical meaning beyond our perception, has come at length to believe there is no such fixed center towards which our searchings strive. Existentialism is, thus, the dull receding roar of classicism and rationalism while structuralism is a new flood of the tide.

The difference may be caught through the metaphor of the labyrinth. Classicism had a labyrinth with a center almost impossible to find. One had to get in, find that center and despoil it, and then get out again without being killed or losing one's way. *Theseus has Ariadne.* Existentialism moans that there is no center, or there is nothing in it, or one can't get in, or one can't get out. *Theseus loses Ariadne.* Structuralism says that we create the labyrinth ourselves, that it has no center, that it is infinitely expansible, that we create it as play and for play, and that one can no more consider leaving it than one can envisage shedding one's skin. *Theseus is Ariadne.*

This can also be graphically illustrated from the use of the labyrinth as a central symbol in Jorge Luis Borges (Crossan, 1976). The commentators note, of course, its presence but they have great trouble with its interpretation. Taught by their tradition, they expect it to be a symbol of doom, danger, and existentialist negativity. Yet Borges, they have to admit, seems rather to be enjoying himself with and in it. They struggle with this contradiction but are unable to solve it (Murillo, Lewald, Isaacs). The solution is that Borges is a structural rather than a classical thinker and that the labyrinth holds no terrors for him. It is that which we and he are ever creating around us as the act and place of play and how could one imagine it as having entrance, exit, or central shrine. Its value, not its

terror, resides precisely in the absence of these three classical topographical presuppositions. Their absence is our
freedom.

1.2 Play

> to make a world
> we need out of the reality
> that is
> and is indifferent:
>   but play
> removing us—we must be
>   careful—a point away
> from reality, though
> an uncreated, unspecific
> reality—that is, in a
> sense, no reality at all:
> what *is* out there? beyond
> the touch of what
>   we make?
>
> A. R. Ammons (1965b:25)

The metamodel I am proposing is play. This is my
megametaphor.

1.21 Homo Ludens

My somewhat predictable starting point is Johan
Huizinga's 1938 classic *Homo Ludens* where he defined
play (13) as

> a free activity standing quite consciously outside 'ordi-
> nary' life as being 'not serious', but at the same time
> absorbing the player intensely and utterly. It is an activ-
> ity connected with no material interest, and no profit
> can be gained by it. It proceeds within its own proper
> boundaries of time and space according to fixed rules
> and in an orderly manner. It promotes the formation of
> social groupings which tend to surround themselves
> with secrecy and to stress their difference from the
> common world by disguise or other means.

The book then proceeds to argue that language, law, war, myth, poetry, philosophy, art, and indeed all cultural phenomena have unfolded *sub specie ludi.* The theory is marred most profoundly by two separate but connected ambiguities which derive from a certain failure of nerve, a refusal to take the theory to its logical conclusions. Huizinga vacillates between the historical and the ontological, between proofs showing how culture came *from* play and is therefore successive to it, and how culture arose *as* play and is therefore absolutely simultaneous with it. Two examples. In his "Foreword" Huizinga tells us how his previous lectures on play and culture were usually understood to be concerned with play *in* culture whereas "it was not my object to define the place of play among all the other manifestations of culture, but rather to ascertain how far culture itself bears the character of play." So he had entitled these talks, "The Play Element of Culture" but his hosts always wanted to change the *of* to *in.* Despite this comment the English translator of the book has proceeded to place as his subtitle, "A Study of the Play-Element in Culture." What Huizinga intended was, of course, "Culture as Play." But the ambiguity that starts here is still present at the very end of the book (173) where these two statements are found in the same paragraph. "The spirit of playful competition is, as a social impulse, older than culture itself and pervades all life like a veritable ferment." But, while here play precedes culture, almost immediately this is negated with the assertion that culture "does not come *from* play like a babe detaching itself from the womb: it arises *in* and *as* play, and never leaves it."

1.22 Homo Ludens Revisited

This ambivalence between culture as play and play in culture is of less importance than another problem which has been brilliantly outlined by Jacques Ehrmann in the

1968 *Yale French Studies* devoted to "Game, Play, Literature." This difficulty was already apparent in the definition cited above. Among the various distinctions used to isolate play over against its alleged opposite these two are the most serious: "outside 'ordinary life' " and "differen[t] from the common world." Ehrmann (33) has found the weak spot and he presses on it remorselessly:

> If the status of 'ordinary life,' of 'reality,' is not thrown into question *in the very movement of thought given over to play,* the theoretical, logical, and anthropological bases on which this thinking is based can only be extremely precarious and contestable. In other words, we are criticizing these authors [both Huizinga and Caillois] chiefly and most seriously for considering 'reality,' the 'real,' as a *given* component of the problem, as a referent needing no discussion, as a matter of course, neutral and objective.

Ehrmann joins here those scholars mentioned in the first part of this paper who had questioned the legitimacy of reality prior to and outside of our perception of it. He notes (33), rather ironically, how the term *reality* "evidently needs quotation marks to sustain itself (is it the sign of unacknowledged uneasiness if these authors use them abundantly whenever they are concerned with 'ordinary life,' 'reality,' and all their synonyms?) and to sustain the assault of efforts to question, to define, to analyze—efforts which, to be sure, are never undertaken." His basic contention is that none of these terms can be taken for granted (34): "This 'reality' which is considered innocent and behind whose objectivity some scholars sheepishly take shelter, must not be the starting-point of any analysis but must rather be its final outcome." (I would presume that adverb should be taken in both its senses.) Finally, having used this principle for a careful analysis of both Huizinga and

Caillois, his conclusions are inevitable (56): "Play is not played against a background of a fixed, stable, reality which would serve as its standard. All reality is caught up in the play of the concepts which designate it." Or, even more simply (56), "the distinguishing characteristic of reality is that it is played. Play, reality, culture are synonymous and interchangeable." Reality *is* play.

1.23 *Paradox at Play*

My metamodel, then, is play, but taken in the sense suggested by Jacques Ehrmann rather than Johan Huizinga. And I would note immediately that it is already subject to the two considerations for a megametaphor noted above. First, it is of a logically higher type than its alternatives. This can be indicated by a quotation from the philosopher Eugen Fink (1968:28–29):

> In the history of philosophy thinkers have not only attempted to define the ontological character of play—some have also dared to turn the problem around and define *the meaning of existence through play.* To put it briefly: speculation is the characterization of the essence of Being by means of the *example of one type of Being;* it is a conceptual formula for the world derived from a part of the world used as a model for the whole. The philosophers have used many such models: Thales water, Plato light, Hegel spirit and so forth.

But if I were to complete that final listing as follows: "Thales water, Plato light, Hegel spirit, Fink play," something very significant would have happened. Play is not of the same logical type as water, light, or spirit. It is not on the same level because Fink's play describes his choice of metamodel by subsuming in itself not only the other proposed models but also by subsuming *the very act of all such choices.* When, for example, Thales *chose* water as his metamodel that was no more and no less than an act of supreme play. In mock algebra: it is not that Fink (Play) = Thales (Water) = Plato (Light) = Hegel (Spirit) but rather that Fink = Play [Thales (Water) + Plato (Light) + Hegel (Spirit)]. And if one can think up any other metamodel, would not the act of such thought be easily construed as an act of play?

Second, the paradox involved in seeking a metaphor of metaphor appears quite clearly and at two levels in play itself. A first level can be glimpsed in that piece of pseudo-algebra above if one wonders why it is given as Fink (Play) and not as Play (Fink). Should it be: Player (Play) or Play (Player)? Helmuth Plessner (77) has already reminded us that "Play is always playing with something that also plays with the player, a paradoxical relation which entices us to commit ourselves, yet without becoming so firmly established that individual choice is completely lost." How can you tell the Player from the Play?

Another level can be seen in the micromodel of *game* where the macrostructure of play can be studied in clearer scale. The paradox is our inability to win absolutely without destroying the game and thereby losing absolutely. We quite deliberately establish rules which make *disciplined failure* inevitable. Imagine what a player who always hurled a strike every time he pitched the ball would do to baseball. Or rather, imagine what he would do in the circus to which he would soon be requested to retire. There is no absolute limit to how badly one can play but there is a quite obvious limit to how well one performs. Perfection destroys the game and demands that a new and harder one be invented (Crossan, 1975:15–18).

If all this talk of model and metamodel, paradox and play seems too utterly abstract and impractical, it is salutary to consider the uses to which these ideas can be put, for example, in the clinical treatment of schizophrenia (Watzlawick: 187–256). Sometimes mind can be revealed to us as clearly in its breakdown as in its standard functioning.

1.3 Semiosis

> the mechanics of this have to do with
> the way our minds work, the concrete, the overin-
> vested concrete,
> the symbol, the seedless radiance, the giving up into
> meaninglessness
>
> and the return of meaning:
> [. . . .]
> pyramidal hierarchies and solitary persons: the
> hierarchies having to do with knowledge and law, the
> solitaries
> with magic, conjuration, enchantment; the loser or
> apostate
> turns on the structure and melts it with vision, with
>
> summoning, clean, verbal burning: or the man at the
> top may
> turn the hierarchy down and walk off in a private direc-
> tion.
>
> *A. R. Ammons (1974:49)*

Play reveals itself in communication through signs. This process is known as semiosis, an art whose science is semiotic(s) or semiology. The reason I postulate play rather than semiosis as metamodel has appeared already and will become more explicit by the end of this section. Either semiosis is *mimetic* or it is *ludic,* it either reflects a reality without it (in both senses of the word) or it creates a reality within it. It seems necessary here to choose one's option, to do it consistently, and to follow it wherever it leads.

1.31 *The Range of Semiotics*

The present understanding of semiosis can be summarized by these four quotations from T. A. Sebeok. First (619), on the state of the science: "Even today, semiotics lacks a comprehensive theoretical foundation but is sustained largely as a consistently shared point of view. . . . having as its subject matter all systems of signs irrespective of their substance and without regard of the species of emitter or receiver involved." That statement means that the following ones must be considered as posing rather than solving problems. Second (619): "Man's total communicative repertoire consists of two sorts of sign systems: anthroposemiotic, that is, those that are exclusively human, and the zoosemiotic, that is, those that can be shown to be the end-products of evolutionary series." Sebeok then (619–620) distinguishes anthroposemiotic systems into "two types: first, language, plus those for which language provides an indispensable integrating base; and second, those for which language is merely—and perhaps mistakenly—thought to provide an infrastructure, or at least an analytic model to be approximately copied." He suggests that myth and ritual are basic examples of this distinction. Third (622), while the relationship of linguistics to semiotics is still very much open to discussion, "there can be no facile generalizations overarching both language and the many well identified zoosemiotic systems found in man, such as the territorial, including temporal, spacing mechanisms he shares with the rest of the organic world." Despite this warning, however, Sebeok is willing to hazard one generalization, presumably not facile, towards future research. Fourth, then (623): "it is amply clear even now that the genetic code must be regarded as the most fundamental of all semiotic networks and therefore as the prototype for all other signalling systems used by animals, including man." These four citations will have to suffice as introduction to the present state of semiotic research. Other divisions and distinctions, problems and possibilities (Mulder and Hervey) can be bracketed for now.

1.32 Sign in Semiotics

From the basic semiotic triad of sender-sign-receiver, semiotics has been divided into a second triad of *pragmatics* (sender-receiver), *syntactics* (sign-sign), and *semantics* (sign-?). That question mark proclaims the ontological chasm at the heart of semantics and hence of semiotics, and it is because of this problem that it is necessary to postulate, as I have done, the ontological priority of play over semiosis.

Take a close look at the *sign* itself, abstracting for a moment from sender and receiver, and in three steps. First step. Charles Morris (1971:19–21, 83–84, 416–17) distinguished (20) the "sign vehicle" from its "designatum" or "denotatum." The

> designatum of a sign is the kind of object which the sign applies to, i.e., the objects with the properties which the interpreter takes account of through the presence of the sign vehicle. And the taking-account-of may occur without there actually being objects or situations with the characteristics taken account of. . . . No contradiction arises in saying that every sign has a designatum but not every sign refers to an actual existent. Where what is referred to actually exists as referred to the object of reference is a *denotatum*. It thus becomes clear that, while every sign has a designatum, not every sign has a denotatum.

Hence there is a double distinction of sign//designatum/denotatum.

Second step. Ferdinand de Saussure (66–67), in effect,

collapsed this double distinction *outside* the sign into a single distinction *inside* the sign. "The linguistic sign unites, not a thing and a name, but a concept and a sound-image. . . . I propose to retain the word *sign* [*signe*] to designate the whole and to replace *concept* and *soundimage* respectively by *signified* [*signifié*] and *signifier* [*signifiant*]; the last two terms have the advantage of indicating the opposition that separates them from each other and from the whole of which they are parts." It is clear that the referent, be it designatum or denotatum, has disappeared *inside* the sign. Thus, for example and as a consequence, Roland Barthes (1972:205) can say that "every sign includes or implies three relations. To start with, an interior relation which units its signifier to its signified; then two exterior relations: a virtual one that unites the sign to a specific reservoir of other signs it may be drawn from in order to be inserted in discourse; and an actual one that unites the sign to other signs in the discourse preceding or succeeding it." Interior and exterior relations, by all means, but all are within signs. No mention is made of any relation between sign and referent, however, just between signs and other signs.

Third step. Jacques Derrida (1970:250) has dared us to face the (im)possibility of collapsing even this distinction of signifier/signified. If one admits, as was suggested in the opening section of this chapter, that

> there is no transcendental or privileged signified and that the domain or the interplay of signification has, henceforth, no limit, he ought to extend his refusal to the concept and to the word sign itself—which is precisely what cannot be done. For the signification 'sign' has always been comprehended and determined, in its sense, as sign-of, signifier referring to a signified, signifier different from its signified. If one erases the radi-

cal difference between signifier and signified, it is the word signifier itself which ought to be abandoned as a metaphysical concept.

If we take these words of Derrida seriously we must, at least, consider that semantics involves itself not with the relationship of sign-referent (designatum or denotatum) but with that of sign-system and system-semiosis.

1.33 Semiotic Play

It is the play of semiosis that establishes reality and world for us and, once again, Jacques Derrida (1970) has already made this conjunction quite explicitly. Having defined play (260) as "a field of infinite substitutions in the closure of a finite ensemble," he concludes (264–65) by contrasting the classicist with the structuralist view of reality.

> There are thus two interpretations of interpretation, of structure, of sign, of freeplay. The one seeks to decipher, dreams of deciphering, a truth or an origin which is free from freeplay and from the order of the sign, and lives like an exile the necessity of interpretation. The other, which is no longer turned toward the origin, affirms freeplay and tries to pass beyond man and humanism, the name man being the name of that being who, throughout the history of metaphysics or of ontotheology—in other words, through the history of all his history—has dreamed of full presence, the reassuring foundation, the origin and end of the game.

Hermeneutics, it would seem, has returned at last to its etymological origins as the act and gift of Hermes. But this is now as then a ludic hermeneutics because Hermes is the divine trickster. Karl Kerényi has reminded us (185) that, "like every other trickster, Hermes, too, operates outside the fixed bounds of custom and law." And Norman O.

Brown has written that "an analysis of the oldest stratum of
Greek mythology reveals that behind Hermes the Thief is
Hermes the Trickster, and behind Hermes the Trickster is
Hermes the Magician" (20). Magic, trickery, and thievery.
It is good to know one's ancestry.

1.4 Art

> after these motions, these vectors
> orders moving in and out of orders, collisions
>   of orders, dispersions, the grasp weakens,
>   the mind whirls, short of the unifying
> reach, short of the heat
>   to carry that forging:
>   after the visions of these losses, the spent
> seer, delivered to wastage, risen
>   into ribs, consigns knowledge to
>   approximation, order to the vehicle
> of change, and fumbles blind in blunt innocence
>   toward divine, terrible love.
>   *A. R. Ammons (1965a:52)*

It is the function of art to keep semiosis honest, to remind it constantly that its activity is ludic rather than
mimetic, to hold up to sign-systems their own origins in
play. And just as semiosis uses all possible units which can
be organized into systemic conventions, for example, mo-
tions, colors, shapes, sounds, words, so must the range of
art extend across all these areas.

1.41 Art as Chaos

This position can be clarified in dialogue with the fascinating thesis of Morse Peckham that *Man's Rage for
Chaos* is the origin of art. Over against (27) *"the identifica-
tion of art and order, the almost universal assumption of
aesthetics and criticism and the historical analysis of styles,"*
Peckham claims (80) that "the primary role of the artist is

to provide stylistic disorientation." The claim is worked out against a sophisticated background in semiotics and perception theory which explains very well the constant stylistic creativity and change in art. For example (83): "What the artist constructs are fields of signs: in producing stylistic dynamism, he changes the signs which the perceiver has been using as a means of categorizing the perceptual field as a work of art." Or, again (206): "The categorial reference of artistic 'form' is not to a range of configurations perceived in the artistic field, but to a range of expectations, or sets, or molds, or models in the perceptual set or orientation. If this can be seen at work in all the arts, justification for the hypothesis of disorientation as the defining character of artistic perception will be forthcoming." The book argues this *hypothesis of disorientation* in detail for (124) "four kinds of art: poetry, painting, architecture, and music."

1.42 Chaos or Play?

My disagreement with this most stimulating book might be put summarily by retitling it: "Man's Rage for Play." I can sharpen this discussion by noting two of his words: "world" and "chaos." First, world (92):

> The condition of human life is continuous categorial metamorphosis. We are forever engaged in constructing around us an architecture of categories as fluid and yielding to our interests as the air. There is nothing that man has not sacrificed, including millions of his fellow human beings, in the vain effort to fix that architecture, to stabilize his categories. But all knowledge, all science, all learning, all history, all thought are unstable, cannot be made stable, even by the majesty of the law armed with the power of brutal force. For 'thought' is but the activity of 'mind'; thought is but another term with which to refer to interpretative variability. No language, no sign system, therefore, is isomorphic with

the world, or can be. No sign structure has the same structure as the world.

But I would insist that "world" is already part of and there-fore already inside our language and we cannot talk about it as if it were out there by itself. What does it mean to talk about "the structure of the world"?

Second, chaos (308–315). Once again this is our *word* for what is beyond language, our *sign* for what is beyond any sign-system. Peckham is certainly correct in his argu-ment that art is not for order since semiosis already fur-nishes us with ordered world. It is also true that art by underlining the relativity of any sign-system forces us to a most dangerous and exhilarating experience of the dance of order with disorder, of creation with chaos, and of being with non-being. And, finally, it is marvelously therapeutic and iconoclastic to think of art as *chaotic* rather than as *mimetic.* But we know all too well that the most radical art can easily be coopted into decorative semiosis and that fact must not be pure coincidence. Hence I prefer to see art neither as mimetic nor chaotic but rather as *ludic,* as our play with semiosis and as our consciousness of play's in-eluctable presence within all our semiotic activity.

Art, I would contend, reveals to us both the relativity and the necessity of semiosis, the awareness that while we can play it *this* way or *that* way, we must always play it *some* way or forfeit our humanity. The options are not to be with or without semiosis but to be with or without self-critical awareness of the ludic nature of semiotic activity.

1.43 Art as Illusion

The title recalls E. H. Gombrich's profound and exciting study of *Art and Illusion* which he subtitled "A Study in the Psychology of Pictorial Representation." One could easily imagine a similar book being written for each of the arts, but what concerns me here is how my inaugural paradox of the perceived perceiver reappears in images just as in words. He gives us (238–239) one example from the linear ontology of Saul Steinberg with this comment:

> A drawing hand draws a drawing hand which draws it. We have no clue as to which is meant to be the real and which the image. . . . If proof were needed of the kinship between the language of art and the language of words, it could be found in this drawing. For the perplexing effect of this self-reference is very similar to the paradoxes beloved of the philosophers: the Cretan who says that all Cretans lie, or the simple blackboard with only one statement on it which runs, "The only statement on this blackboard is untrue." If it is true it is untrue and if untrue true.

Steinberg's hand-drawing-hand is itself based on an earlier version of the same image, the lithograph, "Drawing Hands," by M. C. Escher in 1948 (Escher: 69). Thus both Escher and Gödel have recently been studied, along with Bach, in terms of mathematical, artistic, and musical paradox (Hofstadter).

If once we leave the safe havens of mimesis for the dangerous seas of play, we can never escape the paradox of the perceived perceiver and the played player. So be it.

1.5 Comedy

we are led on

to the boundaries
where relations loosen into chaos
    or where the nucleus fails to control,
fragments in odd shapes
expressing more and more the interstitial sea:
    we are led on

to peripheries

A. R. Ammons (1965a:55)

Art lays bare for us the ludic heart of semiosis by the ever-changing variations which force our semiotic activity to its structural limits. And this is the point where Peckham's "Rage for Chaos" has to be reconsidered.

1.51 The Continuum of Play

I would underline again that we have no words for what is outside words and no sign for what is outside signs and beyond semiosis. We have only ones which draw attention to that borderline and that limitation from the inside. Having said that, I shall use [chaos] as the name for the unnamable, the sound for the unspeakable. And I shall suggest that it is both art and comedy which remind us that play is based firmly on [the seething formlessness of chaos]. In all of this I am imagining a continuum whose only differentiation is in the degree of reflexive self-awareness and intensified self-consciousness with which the human player plays reality. I hazard the following diagram as an artificial fixation of this fluid and fluctuating continuum:

the unseeable   *the unthinkable*

COMEDY ⟵————— SEMIOTIC PLAY —————⟶ ART

the unknowable   *the unspeakable*

Two comments on that diagram. First, taboo is our attempt to deny the breaks in the dotted line, our effort to deny or negate the [chaos] which surrounds us. Second, an example. One usually does not appreciate the weave of a sweater (semiotic play) unless it starts to unravel (comedy) or deliberately engages our attention to itself, as in an Aran sweater (art).

That it is a continuum is clear not only from the magnificent achievements of the Winnebago Trickster Cycle,

Aristophanes, Rabelais, or Joyce's *Ulysses,* in which comedy and art have coalesced absolutely, but also from contemporary art where we are no longer certain we are not involved in comedy most of the time. It is quite unclear today whether some of our best artists are putting on a show or putting on an audience.

1.52 Clothes for the Clown

One example of comedy's revelation that semiotic play is but a clearing within [chaos] will have to suffice and it can be seen in the semiosis of the garment system. Roland Barthes (1970:26–27) has noted how the classic Saussurian distinction of language/speech (system/set) is present in clothes as *worn,* but is gradually collapsed in clothes as *photographed,* and even more so as verbally *described* in haute couture. This is, of course, no more than a technical semiotic description of what is ordinarily called the tyranny of fashion.

Think, on the other hand, of how the clown not only emphasizes the playfulness of clothes but pushes this play constantly towards its [chaotic] surroundings. For example, in his very fine study of *The Fool and His Scepter* William Willeford recalls (18–19) how "the misshapenness of dwarfs, hunchbacks, and other grotesques is reflected in the *dress* of the fool, which characteristically contains chaotic and disproportionate elements. . . . In his show the fool expresses both the emergence of form and meaning out of chaos and their reversion *to* it; this reversion has also taken place in the history of fool dress."

In passing, it is fascinating to compare Willeford's interpretation with that of another classic on the same subject written by Enid Welsford (who also wrote a preface for his study) over thirty years before. While she maintains (52) that "the facts of life are tragic, and the human heart is proof against the comic spirit," he concludes (235) that "the fool among us is a perpetual link to the light and the life in the darkness. The darkness in which light and life are a hidden seed is so essential that it must share the value of whatever is most important to us: if the king loves his scepter, he must love the fool who may take it from him. Folly is thus one of our deepest necessities."

1.53 *The Irrational Vision*

That last contrast reminds us of how often comedy has been equated with irony and satire and these then collapsed into forms of moral rearmament. As if the primary purpose and main effect of Aristophanes' plays were to reform Athens or to solve the Peloponnesian War. Were such their purpose, how dismal their failure. But Old Comedy was far sterner stuff than New Comedy. Aristophanes showed us logic and language laughing at themselves and left to Menander the mockery of mores, manners, and morals. Logic: Is it not more logical to ascend to heaven on Trygaeus' dung-beetle than on Bellerophon's steed since the latter requires transporting both food for the rider and fodder for the horse while the former needs only provisions for the rider? (*Peace* 137–139). Language: Note the serene ambiguity of that line which might stand as motto for all his plays: "By words all men are winged" (*Birds* 1438–1439).

Against such a background it is both refreshing and heartening to find Morton Gurewitch subtitle his recent study of comedy, "The Irrational Vision," and to read his explicit purpose (233–34): "The present work is concerned, not with comedy's ability to function as an eradicator of error, but with its ability to utilize and even glorify irrational freedom. I have stressed, not satire, but farce, which like satire sabotages limitations, but not in the service of a logical ideal." And although he insists on a fourfold division of comedy into satire, humor, farce, and irony (2, 9, 232), he studies all of them as manifestations of "the irrational vision" or, as I would put it, revelations of the borders and relations of chaos and play.

2. PLAY AND PLOT

From here on I shall be presuming the validity of this proposed metamodel of play and I shall be considering one specific stream within the continuum of semiotic play whose fluid borders are constantly probed and revealed by comedy and art.

Each section to follow will represent a gradual narrowing of focus: from semiosis to language, from language to story, from story to allegory, and from allegory to parable. But all of this will be understood within the suggested continuum of play.

2.1 Literature

> nothing's simple, but
> should we add
> verbal complexity?
>
> is there a darkness
> dark words should
> imitate?
>   *A. R. Ammons* (1965b:6)

2.11 *From Semiotics to Linguistics*

I do not want to get involved too deeply in the relationship of language and semiosis at the moment. Whether we agree or not that "of all the elements of consciousness and of social life, language would appear to enjoy some incomparable ontological priority, of a type yet to be determined" (Jameson: vii), we should at least have the grace to acknowledge that such a discussion of language is taking place *in* and *by* language and not by any other sign system.

Two examples. Leon Trotsky announced (183) the genetic priority of deed over word by claiming that "the Formalists show a fast ripening religiousness. They are followers of St. John. They believe that 'In the beginning was the Word.' But we believe that in the beginning was the deed. The word followed, as its phonetic shadow." And a very different author, Hermann Hesse, had Siddhartha proclaim (118) that "I do not differentiate very much between thoughts and words. Quite frankly, I do not attach great importance to thoughts either. I attach more importance to things." Neither author seems at all deterred or even aware of the ironic paradox of negating language *in* language. But whether we decide language is simply one sign-system among many, is *primus inter pares,* or is in some way a normative semiotic system, we should at least consider why we are debating the question *about* language *in* and *by* language. We should at least recall the ancient honesty of St. Augustine (*On Christian Doctrine* II, iii, 4) who admitted that "I could express the meaning of all the signs of the type here touched upon in words, but I would not be able at all to make the meanings of words clear by these signs." Exactly.

2.12 Defamiliarization

Victor Shklovsky of the St. Petersburg "Society for the Study of Poetic Language" proposed *the device of making it strange,* estrangement, or defamiliarization, as the principal aim of literature. Victor Erlich (176) describes this theory: "Rather than translating the unfamiliar into the terms of the familiar, the poetic image 'makes strange' the habitual by presenting it in a novel light, by placing it in an unexpected context." Defamiliarization is a crucially important insight of Russian formalism but Shklovsky's 1917 article on "Art as Technique" is quite ambiguous on whether verbal (literary) art must make strange the external *object* (the world out there) so that we can see it afresh or make strange *language* (the world in it) so that we can hear it anew. He says, for example (12–13) that

> Habitualization devours works, clothes, furniture, one's wife, and the fear of war. . . . And art exists that one may recover the sensation of life; it exists to make one feel things, to make the stone *stony*. The technique of art is to make objects 'unfamiliar,' to make forms difficult, to increase the difficulty and length of perception because the process of perception is an aesthetic end in itself and must be prolonged. . . . After we see an object several times, we begin to recognize it. The object is in front of us and we know about it, but we do not see it—hence we cannot say anything significant about it. Art removes objects from the automatism of perception in several ways.

So far formalism seems uncomfortably close to romanticism, for example to Shelley's "A Defence of Poetry" which claimed (445) that "poetry . . . creates anew the universe, after it has been annihilated in our minds by the recurrence of impressions blunted by reiteration." But then when one is ready to conclude that Shklovsky is offering only a new permutation of the mimetic fallacy, he says, and in italics: *"Art is a way of experiencing the artfulness of an object; the object is not important."* In order to avoid any ambiguity, I would rephrase that italicized section to read: Art is a way of experiencing the artfulness of language; the object is linguistic. Defamiliarization is necessary to see world-in-language and verbal art consists in laying bare the playful creativity that is the core of all language. But it is clear that Shklovsky's defamiliarization in *verbal* art fits very well into Peckham's disorientation function of *all* art, even if Peckham never mentions Shklovsky.

2.13 The Linguistic Continuum

Literature, as verbal or linguistic art, is part of the linguistic continuum which is itself a stream or a strand, and presumably the most important one, within the overall continuum of the metamodel of play.

There is no question of two languages, one ordinary and the other literary. This disjunction was very accurately criticized in two articles of the special issue of *New Literary History* on "What is Literature?" Todorov claimed (15–16) that "from a structural point of view, each type of discourse usually referred to as literary has nonliterary relatives which resemble it more than do other types of literary discourse," and he concluded, with necessary therapeutic negativity: "Could it be . . . that literature does not exist?" Fish gives a devastating critique of the distinction by noting (1973:44) that "if one begins with an impoverished notion of ordinary language, something that is then defined as a deviation from ordinary language will be doubly impoverished." He is also acute enough to know (53) that "to characterize literature by, for example, fictivity is finally not at all different from characterizing it as a formal departure from normative speech. Both characterizations depend on the positivist assumption of an objective 'brute fact' world and a language answerable to it on the one hand, and of an entity (literature) with diminished responsibility to that world on the other." Fish (52) is also quite ready to accept the inevitable conclusion from these premises: "Everything I have said in this paper commits me to saying that literature is language . . . but it is language around which we have drawn a frame, a frame that indicates a decision to regard with a particular self-consciousness the resources language has always possessed."

I would agree completely with that final statement since the only change across the continuum of play is intensified

self-consciousness. Linguistic art (literature) is language
made deliberately self-revelatory of its playful roots, language kept constantly self-manifestive of its ludic reality,
born of and ever surrounded by the fruitful presence of
[chaos].

2.2 Allegory

> a descent into the subconscious
> (tentacles maybe into the unconscious) is prepared for
>   not by
> blotting out the conscious mind but by intensifying the
>   alertness
>
> of the conscious mind even while it permits itself to
>   sink,
> to be lowered down the ladder of structured motions
>   to the
> refreshing energies of the deeper self: but why is it of
>   use
>
> to be brought through organized motion from chaos
>   and
> ephemerality to no-motion: to touch the knowledge
>   that
> motions are instances of order and direction occurring
>
> briefly in the stillness that surrounds
> _A. R. Ammons (1974:40–41)_

This section is another narrowing of focus. Allegory is
considered as a special phenomenon or _technique_ (in the
Russian formalist sense of that term) within the linguistic
sub-continuum of semiotic play.

2.21 _Story as Literature_

I am leaving aside within literature or linguistic art both
the ludic self-manifestivity of poetry (Jakobson) and also

that of prose (a peasant disappearing into a bush?) literature which lies outside the rubric of narrative or story as
art.

Once again I begin with a Russian formalist, this time
Boris Tomashevsky (66–67) of the Moscow Linguistic Cir-
cle. He suggested a crucial distinction between story
(*fabula*) and plot (*sujet*). Meir Sternberg (35) has summed
up the difference by saying that "the *fabula* of the work is
the chronological, or chronological-causal sequence in
which these motifs may be arranged; while the *sujet* constitutes the actual arrangement or presentation of these
motifs in the work itself." In keeping with the theory of
defamiliarization or estrangement the function of plot
(think of flashbacks, point-of-view, etc.) is to slow down
our faculties so that we have to pay attention to the artfulness of the story. But, once again, I do not find this to be
radical enough because this *unplotted story* which is the
basis or raw materials for the great variety of plotted ac-
tualities ïs already a plotted minimum, plotted at least according to certain Western theories of time and cause.
What plot actually reveals is that story does not exist, that
there is only *plotted story* and that plot is as necessary for
any story as it is relative to every story. In terms of our
metamodel continuum, plot manifests story as play, as a
special and vitally important technique of linguistic art
self-manifestive of linguistic play.

2.22 Allegorical Plot

Throughout this whole discussion two aspects have become increasingly evident. First, the primordial paradox of
the perceived perceiver has underlined the simultaneous
relativity and necessity of semiotic play: this way, that way,
the other way, but always some way. Second, consciousness seems in perpetual flight from this twofold vision and
for every layer that semiosis lays down, art and/or comedy

has to create a counter-layer, an anti-structure (Turner: 1969, 1974), a "contrary behavior" (Willeford: 82) that reveals its playful existence and its ludic reality.

Plot, I have just argued, makes evident both the relativity and the necessity of story: the former because of plot's manifold possibilities; the latter because of plot's chosen and present actuality. And, as a technique, plot can do this not only in literature itself but also across many other *types* of semiosis, from mime to ballet, from opera to cinema. There is, however, another technique which lays bare the relativity/necessity of plot not only in various *types* of semiosis but also on different *levels* of semiosis. This artistic device or technique is allegory, that is, polyvalent or plurisignificant narration. I shall use the term "allegory" in a deliberate attempt to connect polyvalent narration with the more classical notion of allegorical story (Crossan: 1976).

I presume that allegory does not just mean that this character or that one, this incident or that event in a story can be analyzed or studied within the boundaries of a wide variety of scholarly disciplines and semiotic levels. I understand the phenomenon to mean that the central theme or basic plot or core structure (however one determines such) can be read isomorphically within, say, a philosophical system, a sociological survey, a historical analysis, a psychological study, or an autobiographical confession. An allegorical plot must be able to be read plausibly on the personal, societal, historical, and ontological levels. Or, more classically and more beautifully,

> Littera gesta docet; quid credas allegoria;
> moralis quid agas; quo tendas anagogia.

Which means, in an example going back to John Cassian in the first half of the fifth century, that "Jerusalem" means *literally* the city in Palestine, *allegorically* the Christian Church, *morally* (or tropologically) the human soul, and *anagogically* eternal salvation in heaven. Thus, a story could be read on four isomorphic levels. Without denying that allegory could be used, negatively to protect one's story from the oppressor (Fletcher: 22, 238) or the vulgar (Murrin: 9, 22–23, 168), or, positively, to strengthen it by showing its isomorphism with "nature" or "tradition" (Honig: 12), such (usually) twofold allegory cannot reveal the full range of allegorical plot which is manifested in *fourfold* (therefore *manifold?*) allegorical narration.

Allegorical plot, or polyvalent narration, reveals the play of plot across many levels of reality, personal and social, historical and ideological. And it also makes manifest how certain plots are powerful enough to create an isomorphism for every level of the reality they are introducing to us.

2.23 *Two Ways of Allegory*

At this point is is necessary to emphasize a distinction between classical/medieval and modern/contemporary allegory. I have absolutely no presumption that one is superior to the other. It is simply a question of one's metamodel and of the degree of self-consciousness one can sustain without either narcissism or nihilism.

Mimetic allegory and *ludic allegory* can be clarified in both their similarity and dissimilarity by a few key quotations from the excellent study by Rosemond Tuve.

Tuve suggests two principles which indicate when allegory is present or when allegorical readings are valid (234–235):

> If large portions of a work have to be covered with blotting paper while we read our meaning in what is left, we are abusing instead of using the images. . . .
> The principal drift *governs* the meanings attributable to the incidents borne upon the stream; the latter cannot

take their own moral direction as they choose. If we ignore the stream's main direction of flow, and embark on incidents which travel counter to or unrelated to it, arriving at special meanings for such incidents, we shall presently drown farcically, amid the laughter of the characters, who sit on the bank well protected in the natures the author gave them, only waiting their chance to push us in.

One notes the appropriate way she offers rules for allegory in allegory. And both rules apply just as much to ancient allegory within a megametaphor of mimetic reality as to contemporary allegory within a metamodel of ludic reality.

So much for similarity, now for the far more devastating dissimilarity which can be specified through two more citations from Tuve's beautiful book. I have italicized the lines where the parting of the ways must take place (10, 54):

> It was clearly shared by mediaeval author and Renaissance imitator: the pleasure in pure seeing-of-similitude, taken in as immediately as an echo, while conceiving the literal story, as one sees a pebble under water with more significance than a pebble. Neither water nor pebble offers any great novelties: *what pleases is merely to observe the nature of the world and correspondences one can see in it.*

> For as we take our way without hurry through all the things that happen to him, taught to see allegorically the double meaning of all that he does and all that the others do and say, we begin to read (as though under the flowing waters of events) *a great design, not of the drama-in-men's-minds but of the meaning of men's lives, lying there to be read under a transparent veil.*

Once again I would call your attention to how easily she slips into allegory to discuss allegory. But that is not the present point. In mimetic allegory one is enjoying layers of divinely caused structural order mirroring the divine mind or will. One is viewing with great pleasure, as Tuve says, the "nature of the world" placed there by God to be discovered by ourselves. But *in ludic allegory one is enjoying the playful human imagination creating isomorphic plot as an act of supreme play.* It is, reversing Tuve's correct analysis of ancient allegory, precisely "the drama-in-men's-minds" that one is invited to applaud. I would repeat my insistence that I have no reason to suspect that either view of allegory is superior to the other and I do not think either is less open to transcendence *in its own way.* But I find mimetic allegory closed to me forever and I find in ludic allegory the way I must reread the past, interpret the present, and propose the future. At least for now.

2.3 Parable

        I am
    aware
of them, as you must be, or you will miss

the non-song

in my singing: it is not that words *cannot* say
what is missing: it is only that what is missing
            cannot
    be missed if
spoken: read the parables of my unmaking:

feel the ris-

ing bubble's trembling walls: rush into the domes
these wordy arches shape: hear
        me
    when I am
silent: gather the boundaried vacancies.
                    A. R. Ammons (1963:33)

Ludic allegory is plot rendered radiantly self-conscious of its creative isomorphism across all the levels of world and reality. And when such an allegory reaches the exquisite apex of self-manifestation, I shall term the story that results a *metaparable*.

2.31 *Mimetic Morality*

Mimetic allegory, as everyone knows, carried with it a heavy freight of moral imperative and ethical necessity. Individual and society, past, present, and future, here and hereafter, were harmoniously structured and imposed their order as a categorical imperative upon all. It is probably this equation of allegory and morality that gave both such a bad name and rendered the former so distasteful to much of recent literary criticism. But as soon as mimetic allegory yields to ludic allegory the bonds with this form of instant morality become loosened and a far different vision emerges.

2.32 *Paradox and Metaparable*

The intensified ludic allegory found in metaparable does not furnish an ethical imperative but a paradoxical challenge. At the heart of metaparable one finds, and finds necessarily, that paradox which permeates the entire metamodel continuum, and which I discussed earlier as the permanence of paradox.

Take, for example, the parables of Jesus. It is instructive to compare two recent literary critics discussing these famous stories. Heinz Politzer (84–85) was acutely aware of the paradox at the heart of modern parables from Camus and Beckett and he defines parable as paradox formed into story. He concludes, however, that Jesus' stories, unlike those of Kafka, were not paradoxical parables but carried a clear-cut moral message. Harold Toliver, on the other hand (22), has realized that strange and paradoxical things happen in Jesus' stories: "a radical leap beyond normal expectancy . . . the denouement breaks with deliberate

reason . . . unpredictable crises and a basic discontinuity
between now and then." But even Toliver is not quite
ready to imagine that Jesus might be as radical as, say,
Kafka, so he backs off a little (116–117): "Unlike the
shock of parables like Christ's, [Kafka] rather than leading
to another logic of equal validity but greatly expanded
vista, defies logic altogether and points toward indefinite
chains of reasoning."

It seems that exegetes, biblical and non-biblical alike,
find it impossible to imagine, despite the example of Arnold Schoenberg's opera, the stunning anomaly of Moses
and Aaron: the paradox that he who had seen God could
not speak but he who had not seen could not be silent.
Jesus' parables indicate that nineteen hundred years ago
another Jewish genius took language so seriously that he
applied to it the ancient Mosaic injunction against divine
images and showed to his startled tradition in story what
story could and could not do. Hence, for example, the
parable of The Prodigal Son presents us with a clear and
unsolved paradox: a father gives a special feast for a prodigal son but offers no special feast for a dutiful son. We
shall have to stop considering Jesus as "the greatest master
of the short apologue" (Richter: 13) and see him instead as
its greatest satirist and subverter, a master of paradox and
indeed of double paradox, not a parabler but a metapara-
bler. He who finds the meaning loses it, and he who loses
it finds it.

2.33 *Allegory allegorizes Allegory*

Metaparable is ludic allegory which forces to heightened
self-consciousness the primordial paradox of the perceived
perceiver and the played player. It is this paradoxical core
that makes a story polyvalent or allegorical since it both
invites, permeates, and relativizes each and every reading.
Only violence to the paradox can present a final or official

reading although, of course, "every strong reading insists that the meaning it finds is exclusive and accurate" (Bloom: 69). But this claim is simply part of the play of any extremely strong player. A game, as we saw earlier, can never be won absolutely because it would destroy the play and hence also the player. Therefore, it can be played repeatedly and continuously. So also with the play of interpretation on ludic allegory in metaparable. Since you cannot interpret absolutely, you can interpret forever.

This paradox has one other even more awesome effect. Negatively, it precludes any final or canonical interpretation of the story which contains it. Positively, it turns the story outward as a metaphor for its own very process of interpretation. This is polyvalent narration or ludic allegory at its deepest level. On a superficial level the term could mean no more than the obvious ability of any story to interact with many different systems of interpretation, either Buddhist or Christian, Freudian or Marxist. Such readings could be and often are quite strained and quite banal. But at the most profound level allegory indicates a story whose central structure is a model for allegory itself. Paradoxical parables or ludic allegories are perfect mirrors of themselves (Marin, 1971, 1976) and they represent polyvalent narration at its deepest and most self-conscious or self-revelatory level. This gives us a working definition to consider. *Polyvalent narration at its most self-conscious level is ludic allegory, that is, a paradox formed into narrative so that it precludes canonical interpretation and becomes a metaphor for the hermeneutical multiplicity it engenders.* I would like to retain the term "metaparable" for this most profound and disturbing form of story.

There is a small room in Vienna's Schönbrunn Palace walled with mirrors. Locate yourself in the middle and you will see corridors stretching in all directions as far as the eye can see. You cannot do it with one mirror but you will always see such multiplicity with two mirrors facing each other and you in the middle. Allegory allegorizes allegory, and therefore the corridors of hermeneutic stretch as far as the imagination can reach.

One can assess the parabolic depth, the degree of allegorical play, and the self-consciousness of story by asking, for example, this question: How well does any allegory work as an allegory for allegory itself? In The Prodigal Son, for instance, what would happen if the father is reality, the elder or dutiful son is mimesis, and the younger or prodigal son is play? Would we not have in this story an allegory of allegory and, indeed, an allegory of Western consciousness's path from mimetic to ludic realism?

This question of how and to what degree all allegories, ancient as well as modern, allegorize the process of allegory itself is the far larger problem which now confronts us. Since that question represents for me a future program rather than a present problem, I shall stop at this point. I would append in epilogue a few comments by Manuel de Diégueq (25, 27) who knows full well the dangerous and vertiginous position to which we have come and upon which we now stand.

What meaning are we to give his strange practice? The 'pilot of the abyss' who ties up at the quays of 'reality,' or the dogged collector of tautology who is engulfed in the mystery of the Word: what are their anguishes, their ecstasies, their metamorphoses, their bondages, and what, finally becomes of a word suspended from itself, a word that begets its own curve and occupies a space without support? . . . But how are we now to consider the man of the cosmic gesture? What, under the critic's gaze, will happen to that word which obeys in advance the structure it will give to the world? Who is this strange being armed with the symbolic act and in turn grounded in it, and what will he do with his freedom? What will be his conscience? Is *conscience* to be observed only in the man who strives for the verbal inauguration of the universe? Man of baptism, man the predecessor of the earth, and what have we to say of this latter-day priest, or this, as it were, cosmic condenser who has appeared at the very heart of the unfolding of language?

WORKS CONSULTED

Ammons, A. R.
    1963   *Expressions of Sea Level.* Columbus, OH: Ohio State University Press.

    1965a   *Corsons Inlet.* Ithaca, NY: Cornell University Press.

    1965b   *Tape for the Turn of the Year.* Ithaca, NY: Cornell University Press.

    1974   *Sphere: The Form of a Motion.* New York: Norton.

Babcock, Barbara A.
    1978   *The Reversible World: Symbolic Inversion in Art and Society.* Ithaca, NY: Cornell University Press.

Barthes, R.
    1970   "Elements of Semiology." Pp. 89–107 in *Writing Degree Zero & Elements of Semiology.* Boston: Beacon Press [1964].

    1972   "The Imagination of the Sign." Pp. 205–11 in *Critical Essays.* Evanston, IL: Northwestern University Press [1962].

    1974   *S/Z.* Trans. Richard Miller. New York: Hill & Wang [Paris: Seuil, 1970].

    1975   *The Pleasure of the Text.* Trans. Richard Miller. New York: Hill & Wang [Paris: Seuil, 1973].

Bateson, G.
    1972   "A Theory of Play and Fantasy." Pp. 177–93 in *Steps to an Ecology of Mind.* New York: Ballantine [1955].

Berryman, Jerome W.
    1980   *Being in Parables with Children.* New York: Paulist Press.

Bloom, H.
    1975   *A Map of Misreading.* New York: Oxford University Press.

Borges, Jorge Luis
    1962   *Ficciones.* New York: Grove Press.

    1971   *The Aleph and Other Stories 1933–1969.* New York: Bantam Books.

Brooks, Peter
    1977   "Freud's Masterplot." Pp. 280–300 in *Yale French Studies* 55/56: *Literature and Psychoanalysis.*

Brown, Norman O.
    1969   *Hermes the Thief: The Evolution of a Myth.* New York: Vintage [1947].

Burgin, Richard
    1968   *Conversations with Jorge Luis Borges.* New York: Holt, Rinehart & Winston.

Cage, J.
    1966   *Silence.* Cambridge, MA: MIT Press.

Caillois, R.
    1958   *Les jeux et les hommes.* Paris: Gallimard. = *Man, Play, and Games.* New York: Free Press of Glencoe, 1961.

Calvino, Italo
    1977   *The Castle of Crossed Destinies.* New York: Harcourt Brace Jovanovich.

Carlston, Charles E.
    1975   *The Parables of the Triple Tradition.*
                    Philadelphia: Fortress Press.

Chumbley, R.
    1974   "On Model Building on Model Build-
                    ing on Model Building." *Diacritics*
                    4:15–19.

Crossan, John Dominic
    1973a   "The Seed Parables of Jesus." *Journal of
                    Biblical Literature* 92:244–66.

    1973b   *In Parables: The Challenge of the Histori-
                    cal Jesus.* New York: Harper & Row.

    1974   "The Good Samaritan: Towards a
                    Generic Definition of Parable." *Semeia*
                    2:82–112.

    1975   *The Dark Interval: Towards a Theology
                    of Story.* Niles, IL: Argus Communica-
                    tions.

    1976   *Raid on the Articulate: Comic Eschatology
                    in Jesus and Borges.* New York: Harper
                    & Row.

    1979   *Finding is the First Act: Trove Folk Tales
                    and Jesus' Treasure Parable.* SemSupp 9.
                    Missoula, MT: Scholars Press-
                    Philadelphia: Fortress Press.

Curry, H.
    1963   *Foundations of Mathematical Logic.* New
                    York: McGraw-Hill.

de Diégueq, M.
    1971   "Existential Psychoanalysis of Style."
                    Pp. 15–41 in *Patterns of Literary Style.*
                    Yearbook of Comparative Criticism, 3.
                    University Park and London: The
                    Pennsylvania State University Press.

Derrida, Jacques
1970 　　　　"Structure, Sign, and Play in the Discourse of the Human Sciences." Pp. 247–72 in *The Languages of Criticism and the Sciences of Man: The Structuralist Controversy.* Eds. Richard Macksey and Eugenio Donato. Baltimore: Johns Hopkins University Press [=1978:278–93].

1973 　　　　*Speech and Phenomena and Other Essays on Husserl's Theory of Signs.* Trans. David B. Allison. Northwestern University Studies in Phenomenology and Existential Philosophy. Evanston, IL: Northwestern University Press.

1974 　　　　"White Mythology: Metaphor in the Text of Philosophy." *New Literary History* 6:5–74 [1971].

1976 　　　　*Of Grammatology.* Trans. Gayatri Chakravorty Spivak. Baltimore: Johns Hopkins University Press [Paris: Minuet, 1967].

1978 　　　　*Writing and Difference.* Trans. Alan Bass. Chicago: University of Chicago Press [Paris: Seuil, 1967].

de Saussure, F.
1966 　　　　*Course in General Linguistics.* New York: McGraw-Hill [1906–1911].

Dodd, Charles Harold
1961 　　　　*The Parables of the Kingdom.* Rev. Ed. New York: Scribner's.

Donahue, John R.
1973 　　　　*Are You the Christ? The Trial Narrative in the Gospel of Mark.* SBLDS 10. Missoula, MT: Scholars Press.

Ehrmann, J.
1968   "Homo Ludens revisited." Pp. 31–57 in *Yale French Studies* 41: *Game, Play, Literature.*

Erlich, V.
1965   *Russian Formalism: History-Doctrine.* The Hague: Mouton.

Escher, M. C.
1967   *The Graphic Work of M. C. Escher.* Rev. and Exp. Ed. New York: Ballantine.

Felman, Shoshana
1977   "Turning the Screw of Interpretation." Pp. 94–207 in *Yale French Studies* 55/56: *Literature and Psychoanalysis.*

Fink, E.
1957   *Oase des Glücks: Gedanken zu einer Ontologie des Spiels.* Freiburg/München: Karl Alber. Excerpts have appeared as "The Ontology of Play." *Philosophy Today* 4 (1960) 95–110 = 18 (1974) 147–61, and as "The oasis of happiness: Toward an ontology of play." *Yale French Studies* 41 (1968) 19–30.

Fish, Stanley E.
1972   *Self-Consuming Artifacts.* Berkeley and Los Angeles: University of California Press.

1973   "How Ordinary is Ordinary Language?" *New Literary History* 5:41–54.

Fletcher, A.
1964   *Allegory: The Theory of a Symbolic Mode.* Ithaca, NY: Cornell University Press.

Forestell, J. Terence
1974   *The Word of the Cross.* AnBib 57.
               Rome: Biblical Institute Press.

Funk, Robert W.
1973   "The Looking-Glass Tree is for the
               Birds (Ezekiel 17:22–24; Mark 4:30–
               32)." *Interpretation* 27:3–9 = Pp.
               19–26 in his *Jesus as Precursor.* Sem-
               Supp 2. Missoula, MT: Scholars
               Press/Pittsburgh:Fortress Press, 1975.

Gardner, Howard, and Ellen Winner
1978   "The Development of Metaphoric
               Competence: Implications   for
               Humanistic Discipline." *Critical In-
               quiry* 5:123–41 [*Special Issue on
               Metaphor*].

Gardner, W. H., and N. H. MacKenzie (Eds.)
1967   *The Poems of Gerard Manley Hopkins.*
               4th ed. New York: Oxford University
               Press.

Gombrich, E. H.
1961   *Art and Illusion.* The A. W. Mellon
               Lectures in the Fine Arts, 1956. Bol-
               lingen Series XXXV/5. Princeton:
               Princeton University Press.

Guillaumont, A., et al. (Eds.)
1959   *The Gospel according to Thomas.* Leiden:
               Brill/New York: Harper & Row.

Gurewitch, M.
1975   *Comedy: The Irrational Vision.* Ithaca,
               NY: Cornell University Press.

Harries, Karsten
1978   "Metaphor and Transcendence." *Criti-
               cal Inquiry* 5:73–90 [*Special Issue on
               Metaphor*].

Hesse, Hermann
      1951   *Siddhartha.* New York: New Directions.

Hofstadter, Douglas R.
      1979   *Gödel, Escher, Bach: An Eternal Golden Braid.* New York: Basic Books.

Honig, E.
      1960   *Dark Conceit: The Making of Allegory.* Cambridge, MA: Walker de Berry.

Hoy, David Couzens
      1978   *The Critical Circle.* Berkeley and Los Angeles: University of California Press.

Huffmann, Norman A.
      1978   "Atypical Features in the Parables of Jesus." *Journal of Biblical Literature* 97:207–20.

Huizinga, J.
      1955   *Homo Ludens.* Boston: Beacon Press.

Isaacs, N. D.
      1968–69   "The Labyrinth of Art in Four Ficciones of Jorge Luis Borges." *Studies in Short Fiction* 6:383–94.

Iser, Wolfgang
      1978   *The Act of Reading: A Theory of Aesthetic Response.* Baltimore: The Johns Hopkins University Press.

Jakobson, R.
      1960   "Closing Statement: Linguistics and Poetics." Pp. 350–77 in *Style in Language.* Cambridge, MA: MIT Press.

James, Henry
      1964   "The Figure in the Carpet." Pp. 273–315 in *The Complete Tales of Henry James.* Ed. Leon Edel. Vol. 9 (1892–1898). Philadelphia and New York: Lippincott.

Jameson, F.
1972   *The Prison-House of Language.*
               Princeton: Princeton University Press.

Jeremias, Joachim
1963   *The Parables of Jesus.* Rev. Ed. New
               York: Scribner's.

Johnston, Robert M.
1976   "The Study of Rabbinic Parables: Some
               Preliminary Observations." Pp. 337–
               57 in *Society of Biblical Literature 1976
               Seminar Papers.* Missoula, MT: Scholars
               Press.

1977   "Greek Patristic Parables." Pp. 215–29
               in *Society of Biblical Literature 1977
               Seminar Papers.* Missoula, MT: Scholars
               Press.

Joyce, James
1976   *Finnegans Wake.* New York: Penguin
               Books [1939].

Kee, Howard Clark
1977   *Community of the New Age.* Philadel-
               phia: Westminster Press.

Kerényi, K.
1956   "The Trickster in Relation to Greek
               Mythology." Pp. 171–91 in P. Radin,
               *The Trickster: A Study in American In-
               dian Mythology.* New York: Philo-
               sophical Library.

Kingsbury, Jack Dean
1969   *The Parables of Jesus in Matthew 13.*
               Richmond, VA: John Knox Press.

Lewald, H. E.
1962   "The Labyrinth of Time and Place in
               Two Stories by Borges." *Hispania*
               45:630–36.

Linnemann, Eta
1966   *Jesus of the Parables.* New York: Harper & Row.

Marin, L.
1971   "Essai d'analyse structurale d'un récit-parabole." *Etudes théologiques et religieuses* 46:35–74.

1976   "Concerning Interpretation: A Parable of Pascal." Pp. 189–219 in *Semiology and Parables.* Ed. Daniel Patte. Pittsburgh Theological Monograph Series 9. Pittsburgh: Pickwick Press.

Mepham, J.
1973   "The Structuralist Sciences and Philosophy." Pp. 104–37 in *Structuralism: An Introduction.* Ed. D. Robey. Oxford: Clarendon Press.

Merleau-Ponty, M.
1964   *The Primacy of Perception.* Evanston, IL: Northwestern University Press.

Morris, C.
1971   *Writings on the General Theory of Signs.* Approaches to Semiotics, 16. The Hague: Mouton. Pp. 13–71 = *Foundations of the Theory of Signs* (1938); pp. 73–397 = *Signs, Language, and Behavior* (1946); pp. 399–466 = "Five Semiotic Studies" (1939, 1948, 1956, 1957, 1964).

Mulder, J. W. F., and S. G. J. Hervey
1971   "Index and Signum." *Semiotica* 4:324–38.

Murillo, L. A.
1959   "The Labyrinths of Jorge Luis Borges.
               An Introduction to the Stories of *The
               Aleph.*" *Modern Language Quarterly*
               20:259–66.

Murrin, M.
1969   *The Veil of Allegory.* Chicago: Univer-
               sity of Chicago Press.

Nagel, E., and J. R. Newman
1958   *Gödel's Proof.* New York: New York
               University Press.

Neusner, Jacob
1971   *The Rabbinic Traditions about the
               Pharisees before 70.* 3 vols. Leiden: Brill.

1972   "Types and Forms in Ancient Jewish
               Literature: Some Comparisons." *His-
               tory of Religions* 11:354–90.

Ong, Walter J.
1977   *Interfaces of the Word.* Ithaca, NY: Cor-
               nell University Press.

Payne, P. B.
1978–79   "The Order of Sowing and Ploughing
               in the Parable of the Sower." *New Tes-
               tament Studies* 25:123–29.

Peckham, M.
1967   *Man's Rage for Chaos.* New York:
               Schocken.

Plessner, H.
1970   *Laughing and Crying: A Study of the
               Limits of Human Behavior.* Evanston,
               IL: Northwestern University Press
               [1961].

Politzer, Heintz
1966   *Franz Kafka: Parable and Paradox.* Rev.
               and Exp. Ed. Ithaca, NY: Cornell Uni-
               versity Press.

Quine, W. V.
1978   "A Postscript on Metaphor." *Critical
               Inquiry* 5:161–62 [*Special Issue on
               Metaphor*].

Richter, D. H.
1974   *Fable's End: Completeness and Closure in
               Rhetorical Fiction.* Chicago: University
               of Chicago Press.

Ricoeur, Paul
1975   *Semeia* 4: *Paul Ricoeur on Biblical Her-
               meneutics.*

1976   *Interpretation Theory: Discourse and the
               Surplus of Meaning.* Fort Worth: Texas
               Christian University Press.

1977   *The Rule of Metaphor.* Trans. R. Czerny
               with K. McLaughlin and J. Costello.
               University of Toronto Romance Series
               37. Toronto and Buffalo: University of
               Toronto Press [= *La métaphor vive.*
               Paris: Seuil, 1975].

1978   "The Metaphorical Process as Cogni-
               tion, Imagination, and Feeling." *Criti-
               cal Inquiry* 5:143–59 [*Special Issue on
               Metaphor*].

Robinson, James M. (Ed.)
1977   *The Nag Hammadi Library.* San Fran-
               cisco: Harper & Row.

Scholem Gershom
1973   *Sabbatai Ṣevi: The Mystical Messiah.*
               Bollingen Series 93. Princeton, NJ:
               Princeton University Press.

Schwartz, Howard (Ed.)
1976   *Imperial Messages: One Hundred Modern Parables.* New York: Avon (Bard).

Sebeok, T. A.
1970   "Is a Comparative Semiotics Possible?" Vol. I, pp. 614–27 in *Echanges et communications. Mélanges C. Lévi-Strauss.* 2 vols. The Hague: Mouton.

Shelley, P. B.
1966   *Selected Poetry and Prose.* Ed. H. Bloom. Toronto: New American Library of Canada.

Shklovsky, V.
1965   "Art as Technique." Pp. 5–24 in *Russian Formalist Criticism.* Lincoln: University of Nebraska Press [1917].

Sparshott, F. E.
1974   " 'As,' or The Limits of Metaphor." *New Literary History* 6:75–94.

Sternberg, M.
1974   "What is Exposition? An Essay in Temporal Delimitation." Pp. 25–70 in *The Theory of the Novel: New Essays.* New York: Oxford University Press.

Theissen, Gerd
1975   "Itinerant Radicalism: The Tradition of Jesus Sayings from the Perspectives of the Sociology of Literature." *Radical Religion* 2:84–93.

Thomas, Hugh
1977   *The Spanish Civil War.* Rev. and Enl. Ed. New York: Harper & Row.

Todorov, T.
1973   "The Notion of Literature." *New Literary History* 5:5–16.

Tolbert, Mary Ann
1979   *Perspectives on the Parables: An Approach to Multiple Interpretations.* Philadelphia: Fortress Press.

Toliver, H.
1974   *Animate Illustions: Explorations of Narrative Structure.* Lincoln: University of Nebraska Press.

Tomashevsky, B.
1965   "Thematics." Pp. 62–95 in *Russian Formalist Criticism.* Lincoln: University of Nebraska Press [1925].

Trotsky, Leon
1966   *Literature and Revolution.* Ann Arbor: University of Michigan Press [1924].

Turner, V. W.
1969   *The Ritual Process.* Chicago: Aldine.

1974   *Dramas, Fields, and Metaphors.* Ithaca, NY: Cornell University Press.

Tuve, R.
1966   *Allegorical Imagery.* Princeton: Princeton University Press.

Vaihinger, H.
1968   *The Philosophy of "As If."* New York: Barnes & Noble [1924].

Walker, William O., Jr. (Ed.)
1978   *The Relationships among the Gospels: An Interdisciplinary Dialogue.* Trinity University Monograph Series in Religion 5. San Antonio, TX: Trinity University Press.

Watzlawick, P., J. H. Blavin, and D. D. Jackson
1967   *Pragmatics of Human Communication.*
        New York: Norton.

Weeden, Theodore J., Sr.
1979   "Recovering the Parabolic Intent in the
        Parable of the Sower." *Journal of the
        American Academy of Religion* 47:97–
        120.

Welsford, E.
1935   *The Fool: His Social and Literary His-
        tory.* New York: Farrar and Rinehart.

Wenham, David
1973–74 "The Interpretation of the Parable of
        the Sower." *New Testament Studies*
        20:299–319.

Wilcox, Mary M.
1979   *Developmental Journey.* Nashville, TN:
        Abington.

Wilden, A.
1972   *System and Structure: Essays in Com-
        munication and Exchange.* London:
        Tavistock.

Willeford, W.
1969   *The Fool and His Sceptor.* Evanston, IL:
        Northwestern University Press.

INDEX OF AUTHORS